OUT OF THE S.

A REMARKABLE STORY OF FORGIVENESS AND HEALING

ALISON BUTTENSHAW

This edition published 2019 by Sarah Grace Publishing
an imprint of Malcolm Down Publishing Ltd.
www.malcolmdown.co.uk

First published 2007
Second edition 2012

British Library Cataloguing in Publication Data
A catalogue record for this book is available from the British Library.

ISBN 978-1-912863-10-5

Cover design by Esther Kotecha
Art direction by Sarah Grace

Printed in the UK by Bell and Bain Ltd, Glasgow

ENDORSEMENTS

"Out of the Shadows" is more than a heart wrenching story of one family's experience in the face of tragedy. It is an incredibly inspiring reminder of the power of forgiveness, healing and grace that can truly transform an individual, a family and a community. Alison Buttenshaw's personal journey to freedom and wholeness will give hope and courage to every reader." - **Mark Zschech, Senior Pastor, Hope Unlimited Church, Australia**

"Alison's story is one of unconditional love, amazing grace and the power of forgiveness. She lives her life as a testimony of how God in you is able to overcome even the very darkest of valleys. Alison now lives her life building an amazing family, is a great mum and wife, and is passionate about the house of God. I pray that this book will inspire you to overcome every hurdle on *your* path, which is leading you to your best life." - **Charlotte Scanlon-Gambill, Senior Associate Pastor, Abundant Life Church, England**

"I've never heard a more gripping or horrifying story than what Alison has endured. The fact that she can sing God's praises in spite of all that's happened in her life is a stunning testimony to God's healing power and grace. Readers will not be able to put this book down, but also not be able to deny that we serve a God who is far above any of our circumstances in life, and stands eager to give us beauty for ashes!" - **Shannon Ethridge, M.A, International Speaker & Best-selling Author of the *Every Woman's Battle* series.**

"I've heard many shocking life stories in my years as both a Pastor and a confidant – but none as moving and compelling as Alison's. Her portrayal of the events she witnessed as a child, and her journey of healing over many turbulent years – reveal a woman of great courage and honesty. "Out of the Shadows" is a brave and revealing account, of how strong the human spirit is, in both hiding pain – and then confronting it.

We live in a world where the superficial is lauded and the 'real world' often spurned. But here in "Out of the Shadows", we are all challenged to dig a little deeper in understanding why bad things happen to good people and why good people do bad things. Above all our convictions stands the noble spirit of forgiveness. I believe the power of forgiveness is at the very heart of Alison's story. I am delighted to endorse this stunning book."- **Ps Chris Pringle, Executive Pastor of C3 Church**

READER REVIEWS

"I could not put the book down and wanted to write to you to thank you so much for sharing your story. I could relate to a lot of the things you were saying. Thank you once again!" **Wendy**

"Sad, stunned, amazing, fantastic, blown away, captivated, overwhelmed, blessed, encouraged, challenged, thankful…. the list could go on, but these are just a few words to express how I felt when I read your book. Thank you for taking that step and allowing God to mold and shape you, thank you for not hiding your light under a bowl, thank you for being strong and courageous, thank you for trusting God. So many peoples' lives are going to be transformed through this book!" **Cath**

"I finished reading your book a couple of days ago, it was so inspiring, thank you for being so honest in your journey and so practical in your advice." **Linda**

"You are living proof that life can come out of the darkest place. Your life proves that there is hope. That there can be a future, happiness & true fulfillment for those who never believed there could be. THANKYOU! Thank you for persevering – what a gift you have given! BRAVO!" **Alison**

"I have read Out of the Shadows and it is extremely helpful and inspiring. I needed to fully understand the attitude of forgiveness, especially to never stop forgiving. I have lost the pent-up anger that kept returning. I've learned so much about

how to stay right. God bless you for writing and publishing it."
Danielle

"Just thought I'd drop you a line to say fantastic book, it has helped me deal with some issues from my past and inspired me too. Thank you for being so brave and honest to the extent that it has helped me and is now helping my daughter and will help many more people as a result" **Phil**

"I just read your book! It was fantastic & really helpful."
Michelle

CONTENTS

THANK YOU

To my beautiful mum Jacky - thank you for modelling genuine forgiveness. Your guidance, love and friendship have helped mold and shape me. You are an inspiration and I am blessed to be your daughter.

To my amazing husband Ross - the greatest guy I know! I'm so grateful that God brought us together. Not only are you the love of my life, you're the best friend I could ever have. Thank you for your continued support and encouragement while working on this project and for the years of love, joy and laughter you have brought to my world.

To Kealy and Curtis - you are without a doubt two of the most amazing kids on the planet! You have taught me so much about life and loving unconditionally – without you my world would be incomplete.

To my 'vital friends' – you know who you are! Your friendships have made my life richer than money ever could. This book would not be a reality without you – thank you.

A special thanks goes to Josie Barlow. Thank you for labouring over this project as if it were your own and for helping draw out the best of me. More importantly, thanks for being you – you're an amazing friend and I love you.

Thank you to Rod Baker, Lynda Parish, Cathy Ingram, Jean Carmen and the many others who prayed for me – your prayers were answered.

Last but not least, my deepest thanks go to Jesus Christ, who during my darkest and most desperate times was there. Thank you for revealing yourself to me in such a powerful way and for your unfailing love that never ceases to amaze me. All the praise and glory goes to you!

MYSTERIOUS WAYS

"I asked God for strength that I might achieve,
I was made weak that I might learn humbly to obey.
I asked for health that I might do greater things,
I was given infirmity that I might do better things.
I asked for riches that I might be happy,
I was given poverty that I might be wise.
I asked for power that I might have the praise of men,
I was given weakness that I might feel the need of God.
I asked for all things that I might enjoy life,
I was given life that I might enjoy all things.
Almost despite myself, my unspoken prayers were answered.
I am, among all people most richly blessed."

Author Unknown

FOREWORD

This book will simply take your breath away. If you want your spirit to rise up and overcome whatever obstacles life may throw at you, if you want your life to reflect the grace of God and not the circumstances that may surround you - then this book is for you!

If you met Ali, you would simply never guess the shocking story that lies in her past from the life she now leads. Ali will take you on a journey of how her idyllic childhood was abruptly shattered and ripped apart.

How could one woman come so far through such tragic and desperate events? The answers are within this thoughtful and incredibly honest story of her life.

Ali is not just a "glass half full" person; she lives with the glass completely overflowing with the abundance of God. She is full of life, joy and fun, incredibly positive, faithful and caring. Together with her husband Ross they have created an amazing family with their two beautiful children Kealy and Curtis.

Read and be inspired to rise up and stake your claim to a life of abundance and joy with a God who says, "We can do it together."

John Kirkby
Founder and International Director
Christians Against Poverty

INTRODUCTION

I climb the stairs to the loft and enter my kids' bedroom. I move towards them and watch as the moonlight shines on their faces, they're so perfect. I stand in awe knowing they are God's precious gift to me. It feels like only yesterday that I was leaving the hospital cradling my newborn daughter in my arms and yet now, almost as if it happened overnight, she is ten years old - the age I was when my life was tragically turned upside down.

This thought triggers a series of all too familiar memories. The quick succession of scenes replay in my mind like a thousand times before: images of sexual abuse, murder and suffocating self-pity.

Before my thoughts spiral out of control I consciously make the decision to stop dwelling on the traumatic experiences of my past. I focus on the things I *have* in my life, instead of focusing on what I have lost. I spent far too many years going down the slippery slide of self-pity and know what it's like to be held captive by its suffocating grip. I refuse to go down it again.

It's late in the evening and weary from the day's activities I kiss my kids goodnight and go to bed. As I lay there, I start thinking about the countless blessings I have: a great husband, amazing kids, friends, family, church, security and freedom - the list is endless – what a contrast to how I once felt. I feel the warm gentle sting in my eyes as the tears begin to well up. Slowly they slide down my cheeks and on to my pillow. I cry silently so I don't wake Ross who is sleeping beside me. I'm incredibly aware that unlike so many other times in my life, these tears flow from the deep sense of love and gratitude I feel.

The bible says in Psalm 23 says, *"Even though I walk through the valley of the shadow of death, I will fear no evil, for you are with me; your rod and your staff, they comfort me."* As I reflect over my life, I am truly grateful that God walked me *through* this valley and gave me the courage to find a home in greener pastures.

I know now that the time spent in that valley; times when I felt afraid, alone, betrayed and hurt, God never ever took His eyes off me. He was always with me, walking beside me and guiding me *through* the valley until finally I made it to the other side. Though the journey hasn't been easy, I know I have become bigger, better and stronger! Like Joseph in the old testament, I am able to say, *"You intended to harm me, but God intended it for good..."* Genesis 50:20

Over the years many people have asked me: "Why are you so happy when you've lost so much?" and "How have you moved on from your past?" My usual response was to simply say "it's God!" While this is certainly true, I've realised that for me to help others navigate their way out of the shadows, I need to explore my life in more detail and to identify the Godly principles I have learned and applied which have brought healing and freedom to my life.

It says in James 1:25, *"...the man who **looks intently** into the perfect law that gives freedom, and continues to do this, not forgetting what he has heard, but doing it – he will be blessed in what he does."*

Writing about my experiences and revisiting my past was not an easy thing for me to do. It reminded me of the sadness and despair that once consumed my life and it took me back to those dark and desperate times. But it also reminded me of how incredibly blessed I am to have been set free from all of that pain, and of the great lengths God went to, to bring restoration and healing to my life.

I believe with all of my heart that the principles I learned on my journey will bring healing and freedom to your life too. Regardless of what has wounded you or caused you pain, God understands and He wants to turn that situation around so that it *benefits* you instead of *hurts* you!

Whether you've been through emotional, physical or sexual abuse, abandoned or rejected by a loved one or if you've made wrong decisions in the past – you can be confident that

nothing is too big, too hard or too complicated for God. Matthew 19:26 says, *"...with God all things are possible"* and I know from personal experience that this is true.

If you're not quite sure if you believe that there's a God in heaven who loves you and cares for you, I want to challenge you to read on. You might be filled with doubt and scepticism, but God proved Himself in such a real and powerful way to me that I know beyond a shadow of a doubt that He will do the same for you. The question is...will you let Him?

Since the beginning of creation, God has longed to be in relationship with mankind but He will never force Himself on us. We have to *invite* Him into our lives. So...will you invite God into the dark places in your mind where pain, bitterness and sorrow reside? Will you allow yourself to let go of the things that have crippled you emotionally and spiritually? If the answer is yes, be encouraged, half the battle has been won!

I pray that as you read about my life and the challenges I have faced, you will see there is hope beyond the things that hurt you. I pray that you will seek God with all of your heart and understand that allowing your past to affect your present not only limits the possibilities of today, but it will rob you of the promises of tomorrow! Jesus Christ himself said in John 10:10, *"...I have come that they may have life, and have it to the full."* It's time to start embracing it!

PART ONE

CHAPTER ONE - PICTURE PERFECT

My dad was born and raised in the beautiful coastal city of Newcastle, located about one and a half hours drive North of Sydney, Australia. He met my mum, who grew up in Doncaster, England while he was in London working for the Merchant Navy. They soon fell in love and eventually tied the knot in the early 1960's. With a love for the warmer climate they decided that there was no better place to settle down than in Dad's hometown of Newcastle. They packed their bags, said their farewells and travelled by ship to sunny Australia. Like most young couples starting out in life they were filled with hopes and dreams for the future, and the prospect of building a happy and fulfilled life.

Mum and Dad settled quickly into life "down under" and it wasn't long before they started making plans to start a family. By the end of 1972 they had three children. Andrew, aged seven, David aged four and then me, the baby of the family. I found out years later that I was the answer to my mum's prayers, and not just because I was the only girl. Mum told me that at twenty-eight weeks gestation she went into premature labour with me. Thankfully with medical intervention, the doctors managed to stop the labour from progressing and I was born a few months later happy and healthy.

Our good fortune continued and for the most part of my early childhood I was incredibly blessed. I especially remember in 1977, when I was just five years of age, my dad had an opportunity to go to the UK and work for a year on a teacher exchange programme. Since working in the navy he had studied to become a maths teacher and he was excited to be going to England this time as a family.

During this twelve month period we had the opportunity to travel through Europe and experience many different cultures and lifestyles. I didn't fully appreciate it at the time, but realised later what a privileged childhood I had been given.

When we returned home to Australia, Mum and Dad had plans for their dream home drawn up and it wasn't too long before it was built and we had moved in. Our home was beautiful by anyone's standards: architecturally designed, three storeys with split-levels, five bedrooms and three bathrooms. But best of all it had a fantastic swimming pool in the backyard with fully landscaped gardens. All of this with the added bonus of being just fifteen minutes from the beach and ten minutes from the largest coastal saltwater lake in Australia.

Any person looking at our life or who knew us personally would have described us as the picture perfect family. In fact, for the first few years of my life, it *felt* like we were the picture perfect family!

Memories come flooding back as I think about our family outings with aunties, uncles and cousins. Hot summer days spent swimming in the pool and playing for hours as the sun beat down on our bodies. Picnics in the park and on some days, when we were feeling a little more energetic, we went bushwalking in the nearby Watagan Mountains. But the thing I remember most in the first few years of my life is the feeling of being genuinely happy, loved and secure.

Sadly these feelings didn't last long.

My picture perfect world started falling apart when I was eight. The start of the decline began so gradually it was barely noticeable. It all began innocently enough. We used to play games together. They were harmless and fun to start with, but it wasn't long before they turned sexual. While I felt very uncomfortable with what was happening, I didn't want to tell anyone about it. I would often lie awake at night wondering why it was happening to me. I felt so confused.

Like most victims of sexual abuse, I felt violated, ashamed and embarrassed. I didn't know how to process or make sense of my feelings and I finally drew the conclusion that this type of thing must be normal. While I tried to convince myself that this was true, something deep within me was screaming out that it wasn't.

I tried desperately to understand what was going on in my life, and though I tried clinging onto my picture perfect world, it was fading faster than I could handle. Why me? What had I done wrong? Was it my fault? Night after night I would torment myself with these questions, but I never got a reply.

I began to wonder whether or not I should tell someone, but how would they react, and what would they say? More importantly, what would *I* say? How on earth was I supposed to approach someone? Feelings of confusion bombarded my mind and the peace and security that I once had were now replaced with fear and uncertainty.

As time went by, I became more and more desperate to tell someone what was happening to me, but I was still too embarrassed to talk to an adult. But then I got my chance. I was in class one morning when my 4th grade teacher told us all to break up into small groups to discuss what we had done on the weekend. There were just three of us in my group and I remember very shyly and quietly telling them what had been happening to me.

Their perplexed expressions followed by embarrassed laughter was enough for me to know that what was happening to me *wasn't* normal, and for almost two decades I was silenced by the fear of what others might think of me. I was so burdened by feelings of guilt, shame and embarrassment that I didn't even tell my husband until several years after we had married!

The emotional effects of the abuse not only began to warp the way I saw myself, but the way I saw life in general. Like looking into a shattered mirror, my view of the world was becoming distorted and the clarity and security that I once had was no longer there. Instead of enjoying the carefree days of my youth and innocence, I was lost and bewildered.

I spent the next twenty years living in the shadows of this shameful secret, but thankfully with God's help and with the wonderful support of my husband, I am now walking in complete freedom from it.

According to the "International Violence Against Women Survey: the Australian Component" conducted in 1996, 57% of the 6677 women surveyed had experienced at least one incident of physical or sexual violence over their lifetime. It's for this reason I felt the need to go into detail and unpack some of the key scriptures and principles that helped me find healing and wholeness. These can be found in Chapter Eleven.

I trust that as you explore these scriptures and principles, you too will walk in healing and wholeness.

CHAPTER TWO - ALARM BELLS

Looking back, I know now that there were alarm bells ringing in my family; but at ten years of age, I had no idea what they meant. Even if I did, I would never have predicted the events that were about to unfold. Never in my worst nightmare could I have imagined the complete and utter chaos and devastation that lay waiting just around the corner.

I remember my Dad and my oldest brother, Andrew, having a fist fight on Christmas Day and me being scurried off to my bedroom so I couldn't watch the drama unfold. It was a relief that I had somewhere to escape to, but this relief was mixed with anxiety as I tried to make sense of what had just happened.

Andrew's bedtime rituals of banging his head and groaning to get to sleep are strong in my memory too, but this was always more a source of irritation than a cause for concern.

My Mum and Dad's marriage was also under an enormous amount of pressure after Mum found out Dad was having an affair with a woman from work. The affair had been going on for several months and despite their commitment to work things out, there was no denying the increasing tension in our home.

In addition to everything else, Andrew was preparing for his final year of high school. This is a stressful time under normal circumstances but with Dad being a maths teacher and having high expectations for academic success, a stressful situation became an unbearable one.

Although in hindsight it is quite obvious that these were all warning signs of the trouble that lay ahead - nobody had any idea how devastating the impact would be!

With an increasing amount of schoolwork and the pressure of assignments and exams mounting, the tension continued to intensify. Dad, in an effort to help Andrew with his studies decided that unless he completed all of his schoolwork during the week, he wouldn't be allowed to go out or spend time with the family. This meant that quite often Andrew was excluded from family outings and instead of the weekends being filled with fun, rest and relaxation, they were filled with built-up anger, frustration and time to dwell on these things. Sadly, no one knew the depth of Andrew's emotions or the extreme stress and pressure that he felt...and like a time bomb ticking, Andrew was about to explode.

CHAPTER THREE - 23RD MARCH 1983

It was the 23rd of March 1983 when time seemed to stand still - as if frozen in time. In my memory, it had been a pretty standard day. So standard that I don't recall any of the events that had taken place throughout the course of that day. I vaguely remember kissing everyone goodnight before going upstairs to bed; but that's about it. There were no arguments. No expressions of hostility. No signs of anger. Nothing. Just your everyday, run of the mill kind of day.

But all of that was about to change.

In the middle of the night I woke to hear a commotion downstairs and the terrifying screams of my mum. Initially I thought she was just watching a scary movie on TV, so I wasn't feeling particularly afraid as I left my bedroom and made my way down the corridor. By the time I had reached the top of the staircase however, the sounds had become increasingly louder and I suddenly realised that these noises weren't coming from the TV at all. They were coming from the study downstairs.

A wave of panic washed over me as I realised something bad was happening. Fear and terror gripped me, and with every beat of my heart, I felt the adrenalin rushing through my veins. I felt weak and short of breath. In spite of these intense emotions, I found myself moving quickly down the stairs and towards the disturbing noises. Nothing could have prepared me for the horrific scene that awaited me.

As I turned the corner at the bottom of the stairs there was blood everywhere. It was splattered all over the walls and there was a long trail of blood on the floor. I didn't know where to look or what to do. I wanted to run but I couldn't. I wanted to hide but where was safe? In a state of shock and horror, I continued making my way towards the study where the noises were coming from. As I stood in the doorway, time stood still. My mind couldn't take in what it was seeing. How does the mind of a ten year old cope with such a scene?

I realised as I stood there, that this was not a random intruder who had invaded our family home and was terrorising our family. It was my brother. In the middle of the night and in a moment of insanity, Andrew had taken a kitchen knife to Mum and Dad's bedroom and had begun a sustained and frenzied attack on them. Fleeing for their lives they ran downstairs to try and escape. Unfortunately their attempts failed. By the time I got to the study both Andrew and my dad were covered in blood and I heard Dad pleading for his life and begging for Andrew to stop. In a state of complete bewilderment and confusion, I begged him to stop too.

In that instant Andrew looked up at me, and for a brief moment in time, he was shocked back to reality. Seconds later, looking dazed and confused, he grabbed me and took me upstairs where he tied my hands behind my back with bed-sheets and locked me in the bedroom. I can only assume he wanted to stop me from seeing what was going on.

Fear began to take its grip on me as I lay on the bed with my hands bound. I didn't know what to do or how to get help. I was terrified by what was going on. I felt helpless as I lay there but I suddenly realised that Mum and Dad were depending on me. They needed someone to call for help and I suddenly felt an overwhelming sense of responsibility. In sheer desperation, I managed to loosen the bed-sheets and get out.

I was frantic and ran back downstairs to try and get help. After seeing the horrific injuries my mum and dad had sustained I realised there was nothing I could do to help, other than try and phone for the emergency services. It was at this time that I realised David, my other brother, was also there and we both tried desperately to get through but despite our best efforts, we couldn't. Not knowing what else to do and realising that time was running out, David ran to one of our neighbours to get help.

31

What happened next is a blur, but somehow I managed to find the knife that had been used in the attacks. I don't know if I went deliberately searching for it or if I stumbled over it, but I distinctly remember thinking that if I hid it, then the attacks would stop.

I know in hindsight that the attacks must have already stopped for me to find the knife; but this was my thought at the time. With the knife in my hand, I raced upstairs to our linen closet and hid it under a pile of heavy blankets. Then I ran back downstairs.

Running into the kitchen to try and phone for help again I found my mum lying on the floor in a pool of blood. She had been trying to phone for help but collapsed in the process. I knew that unless help arrived, and arrived soon, she would die. I picked up the phone again and tried desperately to get help, but again to no avail.

The next few moments are somewhat disjointed and vague. I knew the attack on my parents had now stopped and the desperate screams and cries for help were now replaced with an eerie silence. This silence was even more terrifying than the sounds of my parents' screaming, because I knew that time was running out to save them. Never in my life have I felt so helpless, alone and terrified.

Moments later the silence was broken by the sound of our VW Beetle starting up in the carport. I ran as fast as I could to see who it was and what was happening, but by the time I got there, the car had disappeared. As I looked up the driveway for any signs of help arriving, I saw my Dad lying motionless on the driveway just a few metres away. He had multiple stab wounds and I could see that his life was slowly fading away.

Knowing there was nothing else I could do to help, I cautiously walked over to where my dad was laying and knelt down beside him. Knowing what to say in those final moments came naturally. With tears streaming down my face, I simply told him how much I loved him and kissed him tenderly on the cheek.

As I stood up and left his side, a flood of different emotions overwhelmed me: confusion, desperation, helplessness, anguish, torment, sorrow and anger. Never in my life had I been so deeply affected by such a bombardment of intense emotions, and as I walked off into the dark of the night I screamed like I had never screamed before. The cry came from the very depths of my soul and every ounce of energy I had left was exerted.

The paramedics and police arrived on the scene shortly afterwards and I remember looking up helplessly into the eyes of one of the officers. I asked him to help, but I already knew they were doing everything they could. Moments later I was led away from the scene and taken inside to my neighbour's house. While they were preparing for my unexpectant and traumatic arrival, the paramedics and ambulance officers continued working on my mum, trying desperately to keep her alive.

The rest of the night was spent at my neighbours house and the magnitude of what I had just been through started to take its toll on my mind. Not really knowing what to say or do, my neighbours decided to run a shower for me. As I stood there with the water washing over me, both my mind and body felt completely anaesthetized. I couldn't think or feel anything. I just stood there with my eyes glazed over as I tried to take in what had just happened. I don't remember getting out of the shower, what I wore to bed or where I slept that night.

All I remember is early the next morning, walking in a trance-like state towards the fence that divided our house from the neighbours. I lifted myself up onto the ledge of the fence and looked at our house in the hope that somehow I was mistaken. I hoped that what had taken place just a few short hours earlier wasn't real and that somehow it was part of a horrific nightmare. As I peered over the fence, I saw where my dad had been laying not so long ago. I saw the trail of his blood and knew that this was not a nightmare, but a devastating reality.

Nobody needed to tell me that my dad hadn't survived the attack. Something within me already knew that. As I stood there peering over the fence, I felt the presence of death take a hold of me, and though I wanted to run and scream, I couldn't - I was simply too exhausted.

Climbing back down off the fence I started walking back to the house. My very anxious neighbour, who was obviously concerned by the fact that I was looking at the crime scene, met me. She knew that this scene would be disturbing for the toughest of professionals and naturally wanted to protect me from being even more traumatised. She gently put her arms around me and led me back inside.

CHAPTER FOUR - AFTERMATH

With Dad having passed away and mum critically injured in hospital, my brother David and I were separated and cared for by different aunties and uncles. This was only a short-term arrangement while Mum was in hospital recovering, and even though I understood she needed to be there, I missed her and wanted to be with her.

Just days after the attack I visited Mum in hospital for the first time. She was in the Intensive Care Unit and I remember feeling petrified by the strange smells and beeping sounds of the machines that were helping to keep her alive. For the first few moments I actually struggled to believe that this was my mum lying before me because she was literally covered in bandages. I sat there not really knowing what to say or do, but at the same time, I also knew that it didn't really matter. She was alive and because of that, I felt safe.

Although it felt like Mum was in hospital for an eternity, she was actually only there for a couple of months. As her condition began to improve and she was moved from the Intensive Care Unit to the general ward, my fear of visiting was soon replaced with excitement. These hospital visits became the highlight of my week and I spent hours making "get well" cards and collecting shells from the lakeside so I could make her special homemade necklaces. I was so happy that she had survived.

As the weeks and months passed Mum, David and I were reunited as a family. We started to rebuild our lives and tried to return to a somewhat "normal" existence. Despite our best efforts though, we were constantly reminded of our very tragic past. There were times when the six o'clock news would bring the latest update on the murder case and I would feel the tension in the room rise as the three of us sat watching it. Seeing our lives being broadcast for all to see was horrible and I remember Mum asking us to change the channel over - which we were always willing to do.

A few months later I had to testify against Andrew in court and was made to relive the events that had taken place on that tragic day. This was particularly hard for me as I was still struggling to come to terms with the death of my dad and my brother being the perpetrator, let alone having to give a detailed account to dozens of strangers who were listening and writing down every single word that was spoken.

After the trial was over, Andrew was sentenced to four years in a juvenile home. Not a very lengthy sentence when you consider the nature of the crime that was committed, but the judge had three reasons for handing down this sentence. The first one was that Andrew was only seventeen at the time of the attack and was therefore tried as a juvenile. The second was that he had confidence that Andrew would never re-offend, and the third was that he knew Andrew was remorseful and would have to live with the consequences of his actions for the rest of his life.

With the trial now over, we were left to get on with "normal" life. But what was normal? How were we supposed to move on after such tragedy?

I don't really know how Mum or David dealt with their emotions, but I began to withdraw and isolate myself even more so than before. My security in the world was utterly destroyed and I felt that the only way to protect myself was to disengage from everyone and everything around me. While I still went through the motions of interacting with people and activities, emotionally I had shut down and went to great lengths to conceal my real feelings and thoughts.

As time went by this became an ever-increasing problem for me, but instead of seeking help, I became even more isolated. I would torment myself with questions that had no answers, and bottle up emotions until I snapped and expressed them through anger.

Over time I became increasingly concerned by my apparent inability to control my emotions to the point where I actually scared myself. The first time this happened was shortly after my mum bought us a cocker spaniel puppy, called Rusty.

I have no doubt that Mum bought Rusty to help distract us from the trauma of what we had been through. Whilst this was a great idea and initially provided me with an outlet for love and affection, when Rusty failed to respond to me or didn't reciprocate my love, I would get angry - really angry! I remember one time being so infuriated by Rusty's apparent rejection that I picked him up and hurled him across the backyard. After hitting the ground with a thud and rolling several metres, he ran away yelping and cowered in the garden.

These outbursts of anger really concerned me and I began to wonder if I had the same capabilities that my brother had. I often went to bed feeling ashamed of my behaviour and desperate to gain control of these outbursts but I had no idea of how. I simply concluded that anger was in my genes, that I was a horrible person and unworthy of love and affection. Unfortunately these outbursts were to become more and more evident in my life as time progressed, and it wasn't until I had been married for several years, that I felt fully equipped to deal with them.

Being all too aware of the trauma that we had been exposed to and having concerns for the emotional damage done, Mum made an appointment for David and me to see a psychiatrist for counselling. Despite my hesitation, I reluctantly agreed. I don't remember much about what was said at the time, but the psychiatrist afterwards didn't feel that I was in need of ongoing therapy. All he said was that I might require professional help in the future and that it was difficult to predict when.

Apart from the outbursts of rage that surfaced from time to time, I managed to suppress all of the other emotions pretty effectively. By the time I was thirteen, I was managing to live a relatively normal lifestyle. I was having sleepovers with friends, had crushes on boys, and got into mischief like most other kids my age.

Some say that ignorance is bliss, and whilst I had managed to ignore my past and suppress the suffocating emotions for three years, I was aware that doing so was becoming increasingly difficult to do.

CHAPTER FIVE - FEAR AND CONFUSION

As I grew older, I found myself growing more unsettled and restless. I was increasingly frustrated not only with myself, but also with life in general. The raw emotions that I had somehow managed to contain and suppress were now slowly making their way to the surface.

When I was around my family and friends, I hid behind a bright, happy and outgoing personality and acted like nothing in the world concerned me. However, when I was by myself, I was consumed with fear, anxiety and confusion.

As each day drew to a close and night fell, I could feel my stomach churning over and over. My fun filled days at school turned into nights of panic and fear. As I sat around watching TV with my mum and brother I would try desperately to fight these anxious feelings and thoughts. But I couldn't. I knew that as soon as I went to bed I would have to contend with the demons of my past as well as the flashbacks and memories that were tormenting my mind on a regular basis.

These episodes would often turn into full-blown panic attacks and I would lie in the still of the night being completely paralysed with fear. In hindsight, I now know that I was suffering from Post-Traumatic Stress Disorder (PTSD), but at the time I had never heard of such a diagnosis. This lack of understanding, combined with my raging emotions, contributed to the confusion that I was experiencing.

On some occasions, when I just couldn't bear the torment anymore, I would crawl on my hands and knees into Mum's bedroom. Curling into a ball on the floor beside her bed, I would try desperately to fall asleep. Despite not having the comfort of a bed, I somehow felt so much better just being close to her. On the odd occasion Mum would wake up in the morning, confused to find me lying on the floor but whenever she enquired, I would make up some poor excuse for my bizarre behaviour. Besides, how could I explain it to her when I didn't fully understand it myself?

These panic attacks became more and more frequent as I got older and by the time I was about fourteen they had become a part of my daily life. On some mornings I would be walking to the bus stop to get to school and be so overcome by fear that I would stop mid stride – paralysed. I was too scared to move forward but terrified to go back. After a few minutes, knowing full-well I couldn't stand there all day frozen with fear, I would literally force myself to put one foot in front of the other to keep moving. More often than not, by the time I actually caught the bus, my fear had subsided and I felt okay again.

As the years passed, things continued to deteriorate for me both emotionally and circumstantially. A massive division had taken place in our extended family and this added more confusion and heartache to my life.

While Mum had decided to forgive Andrew for what he had done, some relatives who I loved dearly, couldn't. Instead of accepting Mum's decision to walk in forgiveness, they allowed bitterness to enter their hearts. This bitterness was not just aimed towards Andrew, but to any member of our family who was willing to forgive him.

Even though I completely understood these feelings of bitterness and anger and felt they were "justified", I couldn't help but feel let down and hurt by the hostilities that were arising. All I wanted was for everyone to lay their differing opinions aside and protect the remnants of our family. As time went by though, it became more obvious that this wasn't going to happen. I not only had to come to terms with the traumatic loss of my dad, but now the loss of my much-loved aunts, uncles and cousins as well.

Over the next few years, amongst all the pain and turmoil, I continued to search for understanding and purpose for my life - but there were no answers to the ongoing questions. Life had lost all of its meaning for me and my world began to spiral quickly out of control. I felt like I was sinking in quicksand, and there was no one equipped to help or pull me out of it.

To help try and numb my feelings, I turned to binge drinking and the use of drugs. I figured if I couldn't get rid of the pain, then the least I could do was desensitize myself to it. If I was lucky I would wake the next morning after a big night out, safe at someone's house, but there were countless occasions when I literally woke in the gutter left wondering what on earth had happened the night before.

I remember once staggering down to the beach in the early hours of the morning after a particular big night in town. As I sat there I watched one of the most beautiful sunrises I had ever seen. I sat for hours captivated by the beauty of the sun as it rose above the horizon, fascinated by the array of colours.

It was here, for the first time, that I started seriously asking questions about the meaning of life and if there was any real purpose behind it. Sitting on that beach, I had a good hard look at my life and realised how desperately unhappy I was. The reality of it felt like a slap across the face. While this was a defining moment for me, I had a long way to go before I found the answer that my heart was searching and longing for.

By the time I was sixteen I had well and truly lost all interest in school. To be more specific, I had lost all interest in getting an education. I saw little or no point in studying for hours on end when as far as I was concerned, the future held nothing for me. School had purely become a meeting place where I could hang out with my friends and escape the torment in my mind.

Not surprisingly, this attitude I held towards school became an increasing frustration to my mum. She grew sick and tired of hearing about the detentions I was getting, especially in light of the fact that she was paying an extortionate sum of money for the privilege of a private education. It wasn't only Mum who was disappointed with my attitude; my teachers had also grown tired of my chatty and disruptive behaviour. Instead of having me in the classroom, they preferred me standing in the hallway where I would prove much less of a distraction to my friends.

While many of my teachers were frustrated with my behaviour in class, there was one in particular who stands out in my mind. She was my Year 7 science teacher. After returning to school after the summer holidays, Miss Marshall humiliated me by making me stand up in front of the entire class. Telling me to turn around full circle, she proceeded to point out to everyone how much weight I had gained. To this day, I'm not sure if it was to pay me back for being disruptive in class or if she just simply didn't like me. One thing I do know is that I will never forget how embarrassed and humiliated her comments made me feel.

Because of the reputation I had created for myself at school, my mum finally decided that it might be helpful to start afresh in a different school. While this had always been used as a threat in the past, it was now a reality and although I was unhappy with the decision, I understood her reasoning behind it. After all, why should she spend thousands of dollars a term for me to have a great social life? Unfortunately this "understanding" didn't make the transition any easier, and I enrolled in my new school with a massive "chip on my shoulder", and an attitude that had grown even worse than before.

Desperately unhappy with my new set of circumstances and still struggling with the emotions that were raging inside of me, I began to obsess about my appearance and weight. Sadly this is not uncommon amongst teenagers, but for me it was intensified because of the previous comments about my weight. Before long I had begun to regularly restrict my calorie intake to only 100 calories a day and thought that if I lost weight, this teacher would be proved wrong.

While I knew this was not a sustainable intake of calories needed to be healthy, I couldn't help but beat myself up when I gave in to the desire to eat normally. I would be so angry with myself for giving in and for being weak willed that I would immediately go to the bathroom and make myself sick. Sadly, I spent the next several years living in bondage to this eating pattern, and it wasn't until I was almost twenty that I was delivered from it.

During these dark and desperate times I was completely oblivious to how self-destructive and disconnected to life I had become. I just didn't seem to care about anything anymore and my actions were beginning to reflect that as I became more careless and reckless.

Most people, including my friends, were completely unaware of this secret life I was living behind closed doors; though at times they probably suspected that something wasn't quite right.

I distinctly remember collapsing at a party one night and repeatedly telling my friend that I wished I were dead. My friend was distressed when she saw how unhappy I was but there was nothing she could say or do to ease my pain. The reality was, I didn't really want to die, I just wanted all the pain and heartache to end. I just wanted to have hope that I wouldn't be in a constant state of torment forever.

It was during these desperate and dark times that I grew increasingly aware of the need for change in my life. I knew that unless this change came soon, I might cross the point of no return and find it difficult to drag myself out of the sinking sand that I was getting further and further drawn into.

Thankfully the change I needed was just around the corner.

CHAPTER SIX — A BETTER WAY

It wasn't until the second and final year at my new high school, that I finally allowed some acquaintances to turn into friendships. Instead of resenting my peers and pushing them away, I began to see the positive aspects of these friendships and started to embrace them.

There was one small group that I particularly enjoyed spending time with. We were all in similar classes and it wasn't long before we became a pretty tight knit group of friends. At the weekends we found ourselves spending time together and going to the same parties. The more we hung out, the more I felt a genuine connection with them.

Then one day, completely out of the blue, and to my absolute amazement, one of my friends announced that he was going to start going back to church. This news absolutely stunned me for two reasons: the first was that I didn't realise Peter believed in God and the second was that my understanding of church involved two hours of performing religious rituals, and I couldn't imagine Peter doing that. No matter how hard I tried, I just couldn't get my head around it.

Struggling to understand why Peter would want to attend church was one thing, but I struggled more with the fact that he was 100% convinced that God was real. I remember thinking, "Who was God anyway? He never did me any favours, never answered any of my prayers." Because of my own views and experiences, I found it extremely difficult accepting and understanding Peter's faith.

In the months that followed we spent hours talking about God. Peter would constantly tell me about God's abundant plans and purposes, unfailing love, and faithfulness to His promises, while I continually argued that if God existed, why did so many people experience so much tragedy and heartache?

In spite of my negativity and critical attitude, Peter continued inviting me to church each week, and each week I refused. To me, it seemed like a massive waste of time and I'd rather sleep in, than sit through a boring church service. After all, I had been to church services throughout my school days, but instead of helping me "connect" with God, it made me question his existence even more.

Week after week we used to sing the same old hymns and recite the same old verses - none of which made any sense to me. Then men would walk down the aisle dressed up in weird robes, performing rituals that seemed both irrelevant and meaningless to me. I remember thinking to myself that if God was so amazing, as many had claimed, why on earth was His church so dull and boring?

My discussions with Peter carried on over the next few months and they continued even after high school had finished. However, when Peter moved down to Sydney for work, they became much less frequent.

Most of my school friends by this stage had either enrolled at university, moved overseas or relocated out of my area; while I stayed at home, applied for the dole and spent hours dwelling on how sad my life was.

While I enjoyed the freedom of not being at school and the spare time on my hands, I grew increasingly tired of going to the same places, with the same people and doing the same things. As the months went by and the boredom set in, my choices in life became more and more desperate and before I knew it, I was sliding deeper and deeper into the pit of self-destruction.

Being aware of the stupid choices I was making in life and knowing that God had a greater plan and purpose for me, Peter continued to pray and invited me to church whenever he was in town. He had also asked his parents and others to pray for me.

With Peter's continued persistence and patience I finally accepted his invitation to go to church, not because I 'wanted' to, but because a mutual friend had recently become a Christian and also wanted me to attend so I could watch his baptism. I thought that if I was a real friend, I should at least go along and show him my support. So pushing my reluctant and sceptical feelings aside, I finally decided to go along.

I remember feeling slightly concerned by the fact that I now had *two* friends who were starting to go to church, and there seemed to be more expressing an interest. I wasn't worried so much about them actually going to church, but more by the fact that they were all getting involved in something that I wasn't ready for. While I held quite negative views of God and church, I couldn't help but be intrigued by some of the changes that had started to take place in their lives and the new lease of life they appeared to have.

Peter picked me up for church the following Sunday and I walked through the doors feeling a mixture of hesitation, nervousness and intrigue all at the same time. These feelings were quickly laid to rest when I saw how warm and friendly the people were. I was amazed at how vibrant the church was and loved hearing people talk about miracles they had experienced. When I left a few hours later, something within me had started to change. Instead of feeling sceptical and cynical, I felt accepted and filled with a tangible hope that hadn't been there before. For the first time in my life, I thought there just might be something in this God thing and I couldn't wait to explore this possibility further.

Whilst I didn't quite know how to explain my feelings, I knew that what I experienced in church that day felt good. Even though these people were complete strangers to me, they somehow made me feel safe and secure and deep down I hoped they would help me find the answers that I had been searching for.

Despite thoroughly enjoying my experience at church, I didn't want to admit it to Peter. For months I had been arguing the concept of God and putting down the church, and to finally admit that I actually enjoyed it felt like I would be conceding defeat. Even though on the outside I 'played it cool', deep down I was anxious to be invited to church again. When Peter dropped me back home, the invitation came and I could hardly contain my excitement; I just couldn't wait for Sunday to come around again!

Every week for the next five or six weeks Peter picked me up and took me to church. It was during this time, I slowly started to get a clearer picture of who God really was. It surprised me how much I loved going to church and enjoyed hanging out with my new friends, but I still had lots of unanswered questions and hadn't drawn any solid conclusions about God.

One conclusion I had drawn however was that abusing drugs, alcohol, relationships and other vices to anaesthetise my senses was ineffective and I knew that continuing down this path was going to lead to more heartache. I also knew that after years of riding the emotional roller coaster, I was finally ready to put my life in God's hands. I didn't quite know what that looked like, but for the first time in my life I knew I wanted to find out.

Because of my atheistic views, I found this quite a daunting realisation, and yet something deep down within me knew it was a pivotal point in my life. I remember going to church one Sunday and asking people about their experiences with God. It was like I was asking for proof of God's existence. One pastor said to me: "God is big enough to prove Himself to you, you just have to ask Him." I was amazed by this comment. He was the first person who didn't try to 'argue me in to the Kingdom'. He was confident in God and wholeheartedly believed that at the right time, God would prove Himself and provide me with the answers that I needed. This pastor wasn't interested in winning an argument, he was interested in me knowing that God was real!

From that moment on, I started reading the Bible and allowed the things I read to resonate in my heart. The more I did this the more I felt hope rising within me. I started to believe that I had nothing to lose and everything to gain by inviting God into my life.

On the 5th of May 1991, at the age of eighteen, I finally made the decision to become a Christian. I was shown in the book of Acts how all of Jesus' disciples were baptised in full immersion and because of this, I wanted to be baptised too. I wanted to symbolically bury my old life and leave all of the pain and heartache in the past.

Just a few short hours later I was also baptised in the Holy Spirit and spoke in tongues for the first time. Again I was shown in the Bible how this was a prayer language that God wanted to give me for times when I couldn't find the words to pray or didn't know what to pray for. Whilst I didn't fully understand or appreciate it at the time, I knew that this was a gift from God that would help bring radical change to my life.

To this day it remains one of the most amazing days of my life, not because of anything that took place externally but because of what took place in my heart. After living in pain and confusion for most of my life, for the first time since the attacks took place, I felt hope. Hope that my future could be full of promise and potential. Hope that I would no longer live like someone lost in the shadows. Hope that the pain and sorrow would somehow be replaced with peace and happiness.

It's difficult trying to articulate exactly what happened in that moment, but the easiest way for me to describe it is like a divine exchange. I surrendered all of the pain, heartache, confusion, shame, guilt and everything that weighed me down and God exchanged it with love, joy, peace and purpose! I am still amazed and in awe of how quickly I changed from a person who was locked up in fear, anger and confusion to a person that was peaceful, content and confident in God.

The reaction from my friends and family when they found out about my newfound faith was one of immediate concern, but I didn't care about that at all. What I had found couldn't be concealed and I literally wanted to stand on the rooftop and shout out, "God is real and He has a plan for my life." With this overwhelming realisation also came the desire to see other people encounter God. I wanted everyone to know that despite life's challenges and traumas, hope and happiness can be found.

From that point on, I believed that God was going to lead and guide me for the rest of my days. I believed that no matter how fierce the storm or how rough the seas, Christ would be the anchor that would provide me with peace and safety.

For the first time in years I felt like a massive weight had been lifted from me and I no longer had to carry around the burden of unhappiness. I woke each morning with an expectation that something good was going to happen instead of something bad - and I loved it!

I remember reading the Bible and feeling so impacted by what I read. It was as if God Himself were literally sitting down next to me and teaching me the principles that He knew would help completely liberate me from my past and help redefine who I was.

I remember stumbling on the scripture in John 8:31 where it says, *"If you hold to my teaching, you are really my disciples. Then you will know the truth, and the truth will set you free."*

Being free was something I longed for but could never articulate. As far as I was concerned, freedom was something that criminals dreamed and hoped for, not people like me. The more I thought about this scripture the more it resonated in my heart and I realised that even though I was physically free, I was emotionally captive. This scripture showed me that the key to unlocking the prison door was abiding in God's word and holding fast to His teachings. Over 20 years have now passed since God revealed this scripture to me and I'm overjoyed to say that I've been completely set free and delivered from panic attacks. It's a miracle for me to have gone from experiencing these things daily, to not having one in two decades!

Despite the emotional challenges I still faced, I knew deep down that God and the Bible could be trusted. This knowledge enabled me to walk in security instead of fear and allowed me to enjoy life instead of despising it. In Proverbs 3:5-6 it says, *"Trust in the Lord with all your heart and lean not on your own understanding, in all your ways acknowledge him, and he will make your paths straight."* And that's exactly what I did – I chose to trust God!

I chose to trust God in many areas of my life, especially when it came to His views towards me. I chose to believe that

I was His much loved and adored daughter and even though I had lost my earthly dad, I believed that God wanted to be my *heavenly* one. After years of wandering around lost in confusion, I had finally found a sense of belonging as well as a purpose and direction.

Psalm 92 says, *"...planted in the house of the Lord, they will flourish...."* and without knowing it at the time, that is exactly what I did. I planted myself. I went to every church activity there was and I loved it! Instead of hanging out with people who were disillusioned with life, I spent time with people who loved and appreciated it. I was always so blown away by how caring and thoughtful the people at church were, unlike others who only looked out for themselves or wanted to 'take' from me.

I remember going to my first Saturday night youth service which was held in a small community hall. There were about fifty or so young people there and within half an hour of arriving I was amazed to see everyone in the room laughing and having a great time. This was such a contrast to my partying days when a "good time" was defined by how drunk we got!

There was one guy in the room who particularly caught my attention. We were all playing this game and he was laughing so hard that he literally fell off his seat and rolled onto the floor with tears streaming down his face. I was absolutely convinced that he was high on drugs, but I soon realised that neither drugs or alcohol were responsible. It was his faith in

God and relationships with others that enabled him to love and enjoy life so much.

The night ended all too soon and when I went to bed later that night I was amazed at how much fun I'd had. It was as if the good, clean, fun and games that we played had restored some of my childlike innocence, and for that I was grateful.

CHAPTER SEVEN - LOVE THAT LASTS

As the months went by, I found myself getting more and more involved with the youth group at church. Peter had introduced me to a number of his friends and I was relieved that they accepted and included me in all of the activities they were planning. Every weekend we organised something fun to do whether it be going on car rallies, playing games or having progressive dinner parties.

One guy in particular started to capture my attention. He was always the life of the party; he wasn't afraid to laugh at himself and no matter what we were doing, he always had fun. I found out later that his name was Ross - he also happened to be the same guy that fell off the chair laughing on the night I first time went to the youth group!

As the weeks and months passed, we started spending more and more time together and we quickly became the best of friends. Being with Ross was like being in a time warp - an hour felt like a minute and it seemed like our time together was over before it had begun. It didn't matter what we did, whether it was going to the movies, swimming at the beach, or just hanging out... I always had a great time with him.

The more time we spent together, the more things I liked about him. I liked the way he made me laugh and how he cared so much for the people around him. I loved how he always went the extra mile in helping others and although I didn't understand it at the time, I loved that he wanted the best for me - even when that meant challenging my behaviour or attitude. But the thing I loved most of all was the fact that he loved God with all of his heart and lived with honour and integrity. Something within me knew that Ross was the kind of guy I could trust and rely on.

It wasn't long before this friendship blossomed into a romance and to the delight of our friends and family we started dating. Whilst I was excited by the love we had for each other, I was also extremely fearful of commitment - my dad's history of infidelity and betrayal played a huge part in this. Unless I learned to deal with these issues, I knew our relationship was destined for failure.

It was because of these unresolved feelings that not long after our relationship started, I got cold feet and I ended it. It was during this time that I realised, in all of the years that had passed since Dad had died, I'd never let anybody get close enough to talk about any of my innermost thoughts, feelings and fears. Despite having lots of friends, I kept them distanced from my real emotions and I knew I had to let these barriers down if I was ever going to be really happy.

As the weeks passed I really started to miss Ross, not only as a friend who I had fun and laughed with, but also as someone who I confided in and respected. Whenever I had an issue with something, Ross was always there to help me through it and I missed him terribly.

After a six-week break, I decided that I wanted Ross in my life again and was willing to do whatever it took to make it happen. Thankfully, he was equally as willing to give me a second chance and we picked up right where we left off.

Within a few short weeks, we knew that we wanted to spend the rest of our lives together! We chose and purchased my engagement ring, announced it to our friends and families and excitedly set the wedding date for the 4th of July 1992 - just four and half months after our engagement!

Whilst this was a very exciting time in my life, I also knew that it was going to be difficult going into the details of my past. Up until this point, I'd shared bits and pieces but if Ross and I were going to spend the rest of our lives together, I wanted to tell him the details of what had happened in my family.

I'll never forget the feelings of shame and confusion that overwhelmed me as I struggled finding the words to say. It was the first time in nearly 10 years that I had actually verbalised what had happened in my life. The look of shock and dismay on Ross' face was obvious as I shared through my tears. It goes without saying that Ross was deeply affected and saddened by what had happened, but knowing about my broken past helped him prepare for my 'yet-to-be' revealed emotional instability and outbursts of anger.

Whilst many people were delighted that Ross and I were tying the knot, not everyone was. When Ross asked for Mum's permission to marry me, she was absolutely mortified. She was already stressed by the radical change that had taken place since my conversion (she thought I had joined a cult), now she had the added stress of me getting married as well. It took over a week to convince her that we really did love each other and that this was the "real deal." Mum finally came to terms with the idea and gave us her blessing, albeit reluctantly and with a hint of scepticism too!

Up until this point in my life, marriage was something I rarely thought of. In fact, I think it would be fairly safe to say, I never thought of it. I certainly wasn't the type of girl who dreamed about my wedding day or fantasised about meeting my 'Prince Charming', but now that I had met Ross, I could hardly conceal my excitement! I couldn't wait to start our new life together and I clearly remember counting down "the sleeps" leading up to the big day, like a six year old counting down the days till Christmas.

With both of us studying, (I was now doing a secretarial course) we knew that money was going to be tight but instead of holding off and delaying the wedding, we decided to live in a little caravan in the backyard of Ross' grandparent's house. Although it was far from the ideal home for newlyweds, we were absolutely thrilled to start this new chapter in our lives together.

I remember driving past the caravan visualising what our life was going to be like. I believed with all of my heart that our life was going to be blessed beyond our wildest dreams and even though I knew we would face challenges, I also knew that we were both ready and willing to tackle them head on. We were both convinced that as long as we put God at the centre of all that we did, everything else would work itself out. And whilst we were ultimately right, the first few years were full of trials and tribulations. Most newlyweds reflect over their first twelve months and have fond memories of the 'honeymoon period', but for us, our first year was more like an emotional roller coaster. Looking back now, I completely underestimated how much my emotions were going to interfere with our relationship.

I vividly remember one night being in such a fit of rage that Ross had to literally pin me down on the bed to stop me from lashing out and hitting him. As with most arguments, I can't recall what we were actually fighting over now, but I often wonder what the neighbours thought when they saw the caravan rocking from side to side!

Thankfully with time, these violent episodes happened much less frequently and instead of bottling up my emotions till I exploded, I learned to identify the triggers, take time out and then come back and discuss the problem calmly.

One thing that I was particularly sensitive to was feeling inadequate. I often blamed myself for not being able to get through to the emergency services on the night of the attack and felt guilty that I couldn't do more to help my parents. As a result, I would often unleash a torrent of anger if Ross said anything that was interpreted as negative towards me. This anger at times would be expressed through an outburst of words which I would later regret or at times, I would lash out and throw punches. Neither of these methods of dealing with my pain were helpful and I often felt sick to my stomach with regret leaving Ross feeling hurt and confused.

As I began to understand the things that triggered my outbursts, I realised that talking about them and dealing with them was absolutely crucial. Over time, Ross and I learned to communicate exactly what we were feeling. If the situation escalated and I felt I was being misrepresented or misunderstood, (which I often did!) I would take 'time out' to process my emotions which enabled me to articulate my thoughts to Ross after I had 'cooled down'. Helping Ross understand why I reacted in certain ways was vital to the health of our relationship and obviously helped us in our conflict resolution. (see Chapter 12 for more steps on how to overcome negative thoughts, self-doubt and anger.)

Despite the rocky start to married life, I can honestly say the determination to overcome and commitment to tackle every problem has certainly paid off! We often laugh about those early days now and are in awe of how far we have come.

As I sit here writing, Ross and I have now been happily married for over 20 years! In that time we have gone through many ups and downs but ultimately, with God's wisdom and guidance and the support of both families, we have managed to overcome every obstacle and hurdle.

I know how blessed we are to have such a strong, happy and healthy marriage; but it's not just our marriage and family life that has been blessed - it's every area of our life. Whether it is dealing with the issues from our past or dealing with the pressures of today, God has equipped us to rise above every situation and circumstance!

You might be facing a situation today where you need God's intervention. You might need a physical or emotional healing, you might be searching for acceptance and belonging, you might need help with forgiveness or, like me, you might be seeking all of the above. The fact of the matter is this: God has the answer to every question and the solution to every problem!

I will be eternally grateful for what God has done in my life. I am grateful that He knew how to reach me in my time of desperation and He knew that I needed to be liberated and set free from my past. The good news is that He knows exactly what you need too!

CHAPTER EIGHT
FREE PEOPLE, FREE PEOPLE

In 2003, life was going extremely well. Ross and I had continued to thrive in church, in our careers and in our family life. We now had two children after our beautiful baby boy, Curtis James, was brought into the world on the 23rd of August 1997. Whilst everything was going very well, we couldn't help but sense that God wanted more for us.

After several prophetic words and 'God whispers' Ross and I both felt that God was asking us to leave our home, just as he did of Abraham in Genesis, and relocate to the other side of the world. In an act of obedience, we decided to sell our possessions (we kept our house and kids!) and relocated to the UK. This was a major move for us as we both had an incredibly supportive network of family and friends, and also had very 'secure' and well-paying jobs. This security and support however, was never enough to stop us from doing what we believed God really wanted us to do.

We describe this next phase of our life as 'our faith journey'. Our plan initially was for Ross to work as a Business Analyst and earn loads of money while I was going to be a domesticated housewife and help our children transition into life in a different country. I often laugh at how differently God's plans were for our lives!

We knew we wanted to be based in Bradford as this is where we wanted to attend church. When we discussed our plans with our pastors, he explained that this was also where the UK Head Office of Christians Against Poverty (CAP) was. He suggested we get in contact with John Kirkby, the Founder, who would have local knowledge that could be helpful. Ross and I were both very familiar with the work of CAP as our church in Newcastle was the first church in Australia to open a full debt centre*.

When we arrived in the UK a few months later, Ross gave John a call and was amazed at how welcoming and encouraging he was. He even invited us to come and stay with him and his wife Lizzie for a week until we got ourselves established. This was extremely generous especially when they had a young family of their own – including a five week old baby!

I remember arriving on their doorstep with four massive suitcases and two kids in tow (Kealy was nine and Curt was six at the time) and seeing Lizzie stand in the doorway with a huge smile on her face with arms wide open ready to embrace us. Having a warm, friendly, smiley face was such an incredible blessing to me, especially when we had left so much back home. Within hours we discovered they had the same passion for seeing people find Christ and meeting needs in a practical way as we did and we were thrilled to be staying with them.

Within a very short period of time we knew that John and Lizzie were going to become very special friends. What we didn't know was that God was going to use this friendship to help transform a nation.

Within 48 hours John had let us know about some job opportunities at CAP and encouraged us to apply. This didn't really fit into 'our plan' as we knew the salary was going to be considerably less than what Ross could have otherwise earned. At the same time, we both felt that if God wanted to change the course of our life, then this was the perfect time to do so.

We prayerfully considered what this would mean to us as a family and together decided that we would go for it. It was nerve wracking but exciting as we sought God for this new direction in our lives.

We waited with anticipation to find out if we were successful in our interviews and we were absolutely delighted when we got the phone calls saying we would both be starting in two weeks.

I often reflect over this period of time in our lives and am in awe of the incredible blessings that we experienced, not only as a family, but individually as well.

When we first arrived in the UK, we had no jobs, no house, no car and no schools for the kids. We felt incredibly dependant on God to provide these things and so together we sat down and wrote a prayer list. Each night we would pray for our needs to be met and as each day passed, we were thrilled to start ticking things off. God even provided a horse for one of Kealy's friends and I remember her squealing with delight and saying, "Wow, this God stuff really works doesn't it mum!" I truly believe that it was during this time that Kealy and Curtis personally 'experienced' God and I'm delighted that their relationship with Him continues to grow from strength to strength.

After six months of renting, we were able to buy a house of our own and we truly felt that God was blessing every area of our lives. We spent all of our holidays travelling through England and Europe, the kids had settled down and made friends at school and Ross had already been given his first promotion at work.

Working at CAP was such a breath of fresh air! We loved the dynamic, fun-loving environment and the staff's heart to see peoples' lives set free was phenomenal! We had the privilege of hearing about marriages being restored, homes being saved from repossession, children being fed and churches being empowered to meet the needs of their local communities. In addition to this, we heard client after client share their experiences of 'accepting Christ' and being discipled by people in the church.

We had seen this same impact at a local level in Australia but it wasn't until we moved to the UK that we saw the impact CAP could have in a nation. It was exciting to see the centre network grow from 25 centres to 50 in a three year period with a vision of seeing 500 centres by the year 2014. The reality of this vision would mean that every family in the UK could break free from the devastating impact that debt has on people.

The more we heard about CAP's vision to impact the UK, the more Ross got excited about going back to Australia and seeing that same impact there. We did some research and discovered that in 2006, according to the Australian Council Of Social Service (ACOSS), figures showed that one in ten Australians (over 2 million people) were living below the poverty line! Now more than ever there was no denying the need that existed and after discussing things through with the leadership team in Australia and the UK, it was agreed that our time at CAP UK was over.

In 2007, after an extremely emotional farewell to my incredible UK friends, we returned to Australia and started working with the CAP team at the Head Office in Newcastle.

It has been and continues to be an incredible privilege seeing people set free from the burden of debt. Like most things, there are times when it feels extremely challenging but the challenge is far outweighed by the thousands of families who are having hope restored and experiencing true freedom.

Never in my wildest dreams did I think I would play a part in seeing so many lives transformed. Not only because of my involvement with CAP, but because I am now often invited to share my story at churches and other functions.

I believe with all my heart that dealing with the issues of my past has allowed God to use me as a vessel to restore hope to the broken and lost today. My story is now read by hundreds of CAP clients around the world who are facing extremely challenging circumstances and it blows me away to think that God is using me to encourage them. In Acts 3:6, Peter said, *"Silver or gold I do not have, but what I do have I give you."* Like Peter, you may not feel like you've got a lot to offer but the lessons you've learned in life and the experiences you've had can all be used to bring freedom to someone else.

In the Bible, we read of a little boy who had five loaves and two fish, Abraham had Isaac, Moses had his staff, the wedding party had water and an old woman had two mites. In all of these situations, God used what the people had in their lives to bless those around them and He is no different today! Why not spend some time thinking about the things you have in your life and the experiences you've had and how they can be a blessing to someone else?

Shannon Ethridge says in her book, 'Competely His', "My greatest misery has now become my greatest ministry". Whether your experiences have been good or bad, God wants to use them to help other people. Don't waste another second – go out and reach the people God is asking you to!

*Debt centres are run in partnership with local churches who reach out to families overwhelmed by financial difficulties. Together, CAP is seeing people get freed from the bondage of debt and finding freedom in Christ which is something that I'm extremely passionate about.

Mum & Dad's wedding day

My dad & me

Family photo – I'm the one with the budda belly!

Me – aged five

Me – aged ten

Our wedding day - 1992

Family portrait – December 2006

Family portrait – January 2012

Celebrating my birthday with mum - 2011

PART TWO

REFLECTIONS

Just recently my kids and I sat down to complete a 1000 piece jigsaw puzzle. If you've ever completed one of these, you will be all too familiar with the challenges you face when putting all the pieces back together. It's a piece-by-piece, day-by-day process that requires a lot of patience and a good dose of perseverance too.

We spent hours sifting through the pieces and categorizing them into different colours and shapes. The more time we dedicated to working on the puzzle, the quicker we started to see its beauty revealed. It took two weeks from the day we started to the day we finished and boy did it feel good! For a moment I wondered if that was a little of how God feels when He brings restoration and wholeness to our lives.

Our experiences in life aren't too dissimilar to pieces of a jigsaw puzzle. Everything you've been through, even the ugly and painful parts represent a piece of your "puzzle." It doesn't matter how challenging or difficult things might appear to be - if you have patience and determination and allow God to position and use each piece of the puzzle - restoration will come and your life will be complete.

Yes, there will be challenging times ahead. It will require determination, courage, willingness and an attitude that says "whatever it takes", but believe me, you will never regret it!

If you're up for the challenge and ready for the pieces of your life to be put back together then I believe two things will happen. The first is that you will be satisfied, content and blessed by the finished product and the second thing is that others will be inspired to do the same with the pieces of their life too.

In the next few chapters of this book I share some of the key principles that I used to put the pieces of my life back together. Some of these principles can be applied immediately while others may take some time to process...this is okay!

The fact is, if you *consistently* apply these principles, you too will receive healing and wholeness to the broken areas in your life.

So...if you've decided that restoration is what you want, I pray you will be encouraged by these principles and overcome the circumstances that have broken you.

FORGIVENESS

CHAPTER NINE
YOU OWE IT TO YOURSELF!

"He that cannot forgive others breaks the bridge over which he must pass himself; for every man has need to be forgiven."-
Thomas Fuller

My dad's younger brother, Mike not only had to go through the grief of losing his older brother in horrific circumstances, but he had also been given the gruesome responsibility of cleaning the house after the attacks. While he was cleaning out Andrew's bedroom, he found a piece of paper that had been written by Andrew prior to the attacks. On it was a scrawled list of the plans he had made to attack my Mum and Dad.

Knowing the attack was premeditated was too much for Uncle Mike to bear. This discovery made it impossible for him to come to terms with what had happened and his feelings of bitterness and anger became evident to everyone around him. Unlike other members of the family, Uncle Mike found forgiveness unthinkable and felt that it was an act of betrayal against Dad. As time went by he increasingly isolated himself from anyone who didn't feel the same way that he did.

Eventually the bitterness that consumed Uncle Mike created a wall of separation which could no longer be reconciled and we saw less and less of him and his family as time went by. On the odd occasion when I did see him, I was always so aware of how unhappy he seemed. Instead of channelling his emotions to help bring good out of bad, they were focussed in a way that made things go from bad to worse.

The bitterness, resentment and un-forgiveness that held Uncle Mike captive for years eventually took its toll on him. These feelings not only robbed him of his joy and extended family, but I believe they ultimately robbed him of his life. Sadly, he was diagnosed with a brain tumour a number of years later and though he fought long and hard, he eventually lost his fight and passed away.

While Uncle Mike walked in bitterness, my mum chose to walk in forgiveness and refused to live with resentment. Despite losing the love of her life and suffering from multiple life threatening injuries, Mum didn't focus on her loss, instead she concentrated on what she still had.

Even while mum was still recovering in hospital, she was given a day pass and decided to visit Andrew in the juvenile home where he was serving time. I am amazed at the courage, bravery and unconditional love required to go on such a visit. Years later I asked what they spoke about at this visit and she simply said they didn't exchange many words but sat in silence. I have no doubt that mum's presence sent a message of forgiveness equally as powerful as any words expressed. Though I didn't fully understand or appreciate the significance of Mum's decision to forgive at the time, I certainly reaped the benefits of it.

Watching my mum walk in forgiveness helped me see that the tragedies we face in life don't have to rob us of our joy forever. Yes there will be a season of mourning, but there can also be seasons of happiness *if* you learn to cultivate seeds of forgiveness.

Even though Andrew had committed one of the most horrific crimes imaginable, I have watched my mum leave that pain in the past and move on to live a life that has been richly blessed. Now almost twenty-five years after the attacks, Mum is still reaping the rewards of applying this Godly principle of forgiveness. Her relationship with Andrew has been fully restored and instead of continuing to live with loss, she has chosen to live with love.

Though I lived with Mum's forgiveness and saw her rise above the tragedies of life, it took some time for me to fully understand and work through this process myself. It wasn't until I was nineteen years old and preparing for my wedding day that I fully understood the magnitude of my loss. I realised for the first time that Dad wouldn't be able to proudly walk me down the aisle or give me away, nor would he get to hold his future grandkids, or watch them grow up. I realised like never before that I had not only been robbed of a relationship with my dad but I'd been robbed of a lifetime of memories as well. As the reality sank in, I felt resentment and anger rising up inside of me. How could Andrew do such a thing? What was he thinking? As these emotions intensified, I became increasingly aware that they could easily consume me, just as they had consumed my uncle. Although it was difficult, I was determined not to allow this to happen.

I knew that while I had always "gone along" with Mum's decision to forgive Andrew, I recognized that it was not a decision that I had actually made myself. This realisation meant that I could no longer remain neutral. I had a decision to make – would I actively choose to forgive Andrew and live in freedom from my past or would I allow bitterness to overwhelm me and rob me of the dreams of tomorrow?

Even though there were times when I felt justified to hold on to the bitterness and I wanted to dwell on the anger, I knew that living like this would take me down the same path my uncle had gone down and that it would ultimately destroy both me and those around me. Whenever those feelings arose, I made a conscious decision to replace them with positive thoughts and before long, the feelings of anger and anxiety would subside. Whilst it wasn't always easy, I knew that this was much easier than living with the consequences of anger and bitterness. I just had to think of the differences between my mum and uncle to be reminded of this fact.

What I've discovered about forgiveness is this: it's like exercising. Initially, exercising is really painful, but the more you do it, the easier it becomes!

When I first took up Tae Kwon Do a few years ago, my body was in pain for the first few days after the initial training. I discovered muscles that I didn't even know existed and I often felt like I'd been hit by a truck. Now that I am a 2nd Dan black belt and have done hundreds of hours training over several years, I no longer feel that pain. My body has grown used to this type of exercise and provided that I continue training on a regular basis, I shouldn't experience that pain anymore. Forgiveness is no different.

Forgiveness is a choice – pure and simple. You might be in a situation today where you don't *feel* that you can forgive. You might *feel* too hurt, too raw or too offended, but I want to encourage you to stop relying on your feelings! When Jesus spoke about forgiveness, He didn't say we were to *feel* forgiveness, nor did He say we should wait until the pain has passed, or until our circumstances have changed, He simply said, "forgive."

Whatever circumstances you face, forgiveness is a decision that you must make over and over again if you want the pain to end and the wounds to heal. God will bless our choices to be obedient and will often help align our feelings accordingly. I now 'feel' forgiveness towards Andrew, having made the decision to forgive as an act of my will first.

Jesus says in:

Mathew 18: 21-22, *"Then Peter came to Jesus and asked, "Lord, how many times shall I forgive my brother or sister who sins against me? Up to seven times?" Jesus answered, "I tell you, not seven times, but seventy-seven times."* (If you put this in the context of a 24 hour period, this means we need to forgive 18 times every hour!)

Mark 11:25, *"...And when you stand praying, if you hold anything against anyone, **forgive** him, so that your Father in heaven may **forgive** you your sins."*

Colossians 3:13 reads, *"Bear with each other and forgive whatever grievances you may have against one another. **Forgive** as the Lord **forgave** you."*

The fact is this: if you can't forgive others, then God can't extend forgiveness towards you. You may not feel that you have done anything wrong in your life and that you don't require any forgiveness, but the Bible says in Romans 3:23, *"...for **all** have sinned and fall short of the glory of God."*

Notice there aren't any conditions here? It doesn't say that if you've led a good life or if you've been a good person then you're exempt. It says *all* have sinned. If you want to receive forgiveness from God and the blessings that come with it, you need to extend forgiveness to others!

Regardless of what you've been through, whoever has hurt or wronged you, whoever has let you down or betrayed you - forgiveness is possible! There are countless stories in the Bible of people who have been treated unfairly, hurt and betrayed, but in spite of their hurts, they still overcame.

We read one such story in Genesis 37 - 50. This is the account of a young man called Joseph. He had it really tough! Joseph was betrayed and left for dead by his brothers and then sold into slavery. He was then wrongly accused of raping his master's wife and sent to the king's prison. Whilst serving time in prison for a crime he didn't commit, he was again abandoned and forgotten by a person who had promised to help him get out. Joseph spent years of his life in prison with all the time in the world to wallow in his misery and to allow bitterness to take root.

Yet amazingly we read that when Pharaoh was looking for a discerning and wise man to put in charge of the land of Egypt, *no one compared to Joseph*! Why? Because after everything that he had been through, after all the deceit, the lies, the betrayals, the letdowns, the disappointments - Joseph kept God's spirit! He kept his heart pure before God and held no grievances.

What's amazing is that Joseph chose not only to forgive his perpetrators but he also chose to be a blessing to them! Towards the end of the story Joseph says to his brothers, *"You intended to harm me, but God intended it for good to accomplish what is now being done, the saving of many lives. So then, don't be afraid. **I will provide for you and your children.**"* It goes on to say that Joseph reassured his brothers and spoke kindly to them. Talk about going the extra mile!

Whilst forgiving may be hard at times, it always carries a far greater reward than holding onto bitterness. Bitterness is all consuming and will never be satisfied. It will keep you locked up emotionally and will continually rob you of your joy, strength and peace. Even worse, is that everything you do in life will be overshadowed by the bitterness! You might feel vindicated by these emotions but the truth is that the only person you're really hurting is yourself! Lawana Blackwell puts it like this, *"Forgiveness is almost a selfish act because of its immense benefits to the one who forgives."* I love that!

Even though almost twenty-five years have passed since the attacks, I still have the odd occasion when I get angry with Andrew - but I never hold onto this anger. No amount of hatred, anger, resentment or bitterness is going to undo the past, so why waste precious time and energy holding on to it?

The fact of the matter is this – the past is the past, but we all have the power to change the future. Forgiveness is the key that will help you enjoy this future and live in freedom from the things that once hurt you.

You owe it to yourself and to the people in your life to let it go. Now is the time. Let go of the past, reclaim your future and live a life that is rich in God's blessing and promise!

CHAPTER TEN - FRUITS OF FORGIVENESS

"Do not be deceived: God cannot be mocked. A man reaps what he sows." – Apostle Paul (Galatians 6:7)

I understood many years ago that the decisions we make are like sowing seeds – given time they will bear fruit! The type of fruit you harvest will entirely depend on the type of seed you choose to sow. If you plant an apple seed you will reap apples, if you sow tomato seeds, you will reap tomatoes and if you sow seeds of forgiveness you will also reap the fruits of forgiveness. Choosing to walk in forgiveness has not only helped me reap a harvest of great joy and blessing, it has also helped my loved ones benefit from the harvest as well.

This became more apparent to me a few years ago when my daughter Kealy was nine years old. Kealy had on a number of previous occasions asked questions about how my dad had died but I had always managed to satisfy her by explaining that he had died a long time ago. This time when she asked, it was different. She wanted to know the details and she wasn't going to allow her questions to be so easily dismissed like before. The more she persisted in asking, the more I tried to discourage her from knowing. I tried telling her that she was too young to understand and promised to tell her when she was a bit older, but that didn't work either.

Seeing how upset and distressed Kealy was becoming, I decided to tell her, though I kept the details to a bare minimum. As I carefully chose my words and talked about what had happened, I saw the sadness in her eyes and watched as the tears began to roll down her face. I was shocked by her reaction and for the first time realised that this tragedy had not only had a devastating affect on my life but it also had the potential to deeply affect my children, and every generation after me.

I realised more than ever before that if I had chosen not to forgive and allowed my past to consume me, there would have been terrible consequences. Not only would my relationships with family and friends have suffered but the bitterness would have had a devastating impact on my children as well.

Sadly some people think that bitterness can be confined to the one area in their life that has been hurt - but it can't. Eventually it will affect your marriage, work, children and friendships. Why? Because bitterness is like a cancer - it will eat away at you until every part of you is affected.

That night I went to bed overwhelmed with gratitude that I had chosen to walk in forgiveness and allowed God to restore my brokenness and heal my hurt. Though my children have been somewhat affected by the things in my past, they won't have to go through the same pain and heartache that I did. I made sure that my suffering stopped in my generation and that my kids would grow up knowing the importance of forgiveness and living with its fruit.

Deuteronomy 30:19 says, *"This day I call heaven and earth as witnesses against you that I have set before you **life** and death, **blessings** and curses. Now **choose life**, so that you and your children may live..."*

While choosing life over death seems to be an obvious choice, it's amazing how many people don't actively make it. Some people think that being indecisive is the same as choosing life, but it's not. If you don't actively choose life, you are by default choosing death.

This ability we've been given to make choices is called free will and it is one of the greatest gifts God has given humanity. It means that we have the freedom to choose what we do with our lives. We can choose to do good or bad, be wise or unwise, ignorant or insightful, and with all of those choices come natural consequences.

Sadly, we rarely consider the possibility that our children and our children's children could be affected by these wrong choices. The decision is yours. Will you choose forgiveness and life or will you choose bitterness that leads to death? Remember: the next generation is depending on you!

I have since had conversations with Kealy about the tragedies in our family and have found that, despite her age, she too has fully understood the power of forgiveness. She is aware of what took place and how wrong it was but she also understands the damage that bitterness can do. Modelling forgiveness to Kealy didn't mean that she would automatically make the same choice but it certainly made it easier for her. How differently would things have turned out if I had modelled bitterness and anger instead of forgiveness and how differently would Kealy have been affected?

I recently spoke to a friend of my cousin Scott, who was Uncle Mike's son. He and Scott had been friends since they were kids and I was deeply saddened when I heard that Scott had never married, was still living at home looking after his mum and was finding it difficult letting go of the sorrow in his life. It was another tragic reminder, that if we don't deal with our bitterness, we will sadly pass it on to the next generation.

Are there people you love who are suffering because you haven't chosen forgiveness? Are you robbing yourself and your loved ones of a happy and joy-filled future because of the pain and hurt that you once experienced?

There are countless hurtful scenarios that can be replayed in our minds if we allow them to be. The fact is, we've all been hurt and betrayed by someone, at some time. Sometimes we believe, at least for a while, that reacting to these feelings will help us come to terms with the hurt. But instead of making the situation better, it only makes the problem bigger!

While it's normal to experience a wide range of emotions when you have experienced pain, suffering, betrayal or loss, it is important that you don't allow your life to be controlled by them. Don't fall into the trap of thinking that living with hatred or bitterness is a more effective way of dealing with the pain.

I've heard it said that, *"Bitterness is like drinking poison yourself, while waiting for the person who hurt you to die!"* We may not believe this in reality, but there are plenty of people who live like this emotionally. They harbour offences and hatred and convince themselves that somehow it will punish the person who hurt them. My uncle Mike is a classic example of this. He refused to forgive Andrew and yet somehow thought that Andrew would suffer as a result. In the end, the only person to suffer was Uncle Mike and those that were closest to him.

Walking in forgiveness liberates you to live a life full of joy. It in no way means the person who has wronged you "is let off the hook" and suffers no consequences. Consequences are, and always will be a natural bi-product of choice. It may not be immediately visible but as sure as the sun will rise, consequences will too!

Fifteen years after my brother attacked my parents he tried to commit suicide. He said he couldn't live with himself for the things that he had done wrong and felt that the world would be a much better place without him. Some people were appalled at the lenient sentence handed down to Andrew but having to spend the rest of his life with remorse and guilt is a sentence that will last his entire lifetime.

I remember visiting Andrew in hospital shortly after his suicide attempt and feeling overwhelmed with sadness. This sadness wasn't for me but for my brother who was trapped in a world of his consequences. I was so desperate to help him and to take away his pain but didn't know what to say or do. I knew there was no question in Andrew's mind about my love and forgiveness towards him. He even believed that *God* had forgiven him but that wasn't enough for Andrew. What he wanted most of all was to forgive himself!

You might be living with the constant reminder of past mistakes or be living with regret because of poor choices, but you need to know that even though consequences can't be erased, the dream of living a full and rich life is still possible!

There are countless stories of men and women in the Bible who made mistakes but still went on to fulfil the plans and purposes that God had created for them. Moses killed the Egyptian and went on to lead an entire nation out of captivity.

Peter denied Jesus not once, not twice but three times and was *still* considered to be one of his best friends. Saul who later became Paul persecuted and killed Christians and was used by God to write two thirds of the New Testament!

Don't give up on your future because you've made a mistake in your past! God is a forgiving God. The Bible says in Psalm 103, *"...as far as the east is from the west, so far has he removed our transgressions from us."* You don't have to go on punishing yourself! God is well able to forgive and to wipe the slate clean. The question is, are you?

The next time you come face to face with an opportunity to forgive, I pray that you seize it! I pray that you not only see the incredible benefit it brings to your life, but to the lives of others around you.

CHAPTER ELEVEN - FORGIVENESS MYTHS

"The weak can never forgive. Forgiveness is the attribute of the strong." - Mahatma Gandhi

There appears to be a lot of misconceptions about forgiveness. Some people believe that forgiving is a sign of weakness, a passive way of dealing with pain and heartache. Others think that by withholding it, it's going to hurt the one who hurt them – they're wrong!

I see forgiveness *very* differently. I see it as a healing agent - not only to the one who offended but also to the one who *was* offended. Forgiveness is also a sign of incredible fortitude because it takes a lot of courage to confront the past and deal with the emotions from it.

While bitterness, resentment and feelings of ill-will keep you connected to the pain and in many ways tie you to the person who hurt you, forgiveness is a key that can free you from it! Forgiveness will help release you from your suffering and help you live the life that God has created for you.

Forgiveness also has the ability to *redefine* who you are. Instead of being the victim, forgiveness empowers you to become the victor - a person who has triumphed over adversity.

So how can you tell if you have forgiven someone? The Oxford dictionary defines forgiveness in this way, *"To stop feeling angry or resentful towards (someone) for an offence or mistake."*

I believe you've forgiven when you:

- Have come to terms with what has happened to you
- Have peace about your situation
- No longer feel bitterness or resentment
- Can wish your perpetrator well
- No longer blame others for the outcome of your life.

You might not be able to say 'yes' to all of the above yet but don't be discouraged. Remember: God will often bring your feelings into alignment with the decision you make to forgive!

Now that I've discussed a little of what forgiveness *is*, I want to talk about a few things that forgiveness *is not*.

FORGIVENESS MYTH 1: To forgive you need to forget

The fact that you have forgiven someone does not mean you have necessarily forgotten. I made the decision to walk in forgiveness many years ago but I will never *forget* the trauma of seeing my parents attacked, nor will I ever *forget* the abuse that I went through.

Forgiveness should not be measured in terms of "memory loss." It is not a rubber that magically erases the offence that has taken place.

God acknowledges our sin. He knows that we fall short but He doesn't charge it against us. Psalm 103:10 says, *"He (the Lord) does not treat us as our sins deserve or repay us according to our iniquities."*

I believe it serves us well to treat others in the same way. We acknowledge the offense but we no longer feel the need for retribution.

Often I have heard people use the phrase "forgive and forget" when trying to help others come to that place of forgiveness, but I don't believe for a second that forgetfulness equates to forgiveness! I actually think there are times when we *benefit* from remembering an offense!

Take for example a wife that has been verbally and physically abused by her husband. If he apologizes and promises to never repeat the offence but then continues to do so, it benefits her to remember. Hopefully, she will begin to clearly identify the repetitive nature of the offence and take the necessary precautions.

Remembering an offense or a mistake can also help us because it serves as an example of what *not* to do. If we allow our past to educate us about our future, then many of the tragedies that are repeated could be avoided. For example, I have learned from my parents that while school is of great importance, it's not more important than my child's emotional wellbeing. Children need to have an abundance of love and affection mixed with discipline and guidance.

Recalling past mistakes can also help us protect ourselves, as well as others. For example, because I remember the sexual abuse I went through as a child, I am much more aware of the warning signs. This means I can protect my children better, and through conversations with my children, they can help protect themselves as well.

While I believe with all of my heart that there are benefits to remembering the things that hurt you, I can't stress enough the importance of not allowing it to consume you!

If you're still consumed by your hurt and you dwell on it for extended periods of time, I would like to suggest that perhaps you haven't fully embraced forgiveness - but don't give up. Remember, forgiveness is like exercising – the more you do it the easier it becomes!

FORGIVENESS MYTH 2: To forgive means to reconcile

Don't buy into the thinking that forgiveness means you have to be reconciled or reunited with the person that has hurt you. Forgiveness is a decision that can be made by one person, but unity or reconciliation requires the actions of two. There are times when it is right for reconciliation to take place and times when it is not.

Even the apostle Paul chose not to be reconciled to people at times. Acts 15:38 says, *"...but Paul did not think it wise to take him (John Mark) because he had deserted them in Pamphylia and had not continued with them in the work. They (Paul and Barnabas) had such a sharp disagreement that they parted company."*

Here we see that Paul not only remembered John Mark's offence but also chose to be separated from him on a particular mission. We need to get God's wisdom on how to deal with each situation and only you know in your heart what is right for you. Proverbs 4:5 says, *"Get wisdom, get understanding; do not forget my words or swerve from them. Do not forsake wisdom, and she will protect you; love her, and she will watch over you."*

Reconciliation was important to me. I had lost so many members of my family through bitterness and resentment and I therefore didn't see any sense in choosing to lose more. Besides this fact, I loved Andrew and knew that there was more to him than the crime he had committed. For me personally, I saw the benefits of having Andrew in my life as far greater than there were from keeping him at a distance.

If you choose not to be reunited with the one who hurt you, it doesn't mean that you're wrong or bitter or that you haven't chosen to forgive. It just means that the benefits of keeping a distance from that person are greater than the benefits of being reconciled with them, and that is okay.

FORGIVENESS MYTH 3: Forgiveness is not denial

Forgiveness does not mean you pretend that the hurt didn't happen. Living in denial will only add to the pain and will cause the healing process to take much longer.

I love reading Jesus' response to the betrayal of Judas in Matthew 26:20, "*...when evening came, Jesus was reclining at the table with the Twelve. And while they were eating, He said, 'I tell you the truth, one of you will betray me.' They were very sad and began to say to him one after the other, 'Surely not I, Lord?' Jesus replied, 'the one who has dipped his hand into the bowl with me will betray me. The Son of Man will go just as it is written about him. But woe to that man who betrays the Son of Man! It would be better for him if he had not been born.' Then Judas, the one who would betray him, said, 'Surely not I, Rabbi?' Jesus answered, 'Yes, it is you'.*"

Most people in this situation would find it hard coming to terms with the betrayal of such a close friend, let alone having the courage to address it - but not Jesus. He was very upfront and open about it and didn't try to "sweep it under the carpet" or pretend it didn't happen. Jesus fully understood the benefits of accepting it and moving on from it. I love that just a few moments after Judas' betrayal, Jesus takes communion and gives thanks. How awesome!

Another example where Jesus didn't deny his feelings is when his friend Lazarus died. John 11:33-36 tells us that "Jesus wept" and was "deeply moved" by this loss. He didn't harden His heart or pretend that He didn't have emotions. He wept and gave himself permission to grieve, but he didn't allow that grief to stop Him from fulfilling Gods plan for His life. We need to do the same. We need to acknowledge the things that have hurt us but not be consumed by them.

Several years ago one of my closest friends was involved in a serious car accident. She was discharged from hospital the next day with a few cuts and bruises and told to rest up. Over the next couple of days however she developed two black eyes and on further investigation they discovered that she had actually broken three vertebrae in her neck! Failing to identify this injury could have had devastating consequences. One accidental slip or push could have left Danielle paralyzed for the rest of her life.

Recognizing emotional and spiritual injuries are just as important as recognizing physical injuries - perhaps even more so. If you don't acknowledge your injury and live in denial, you won't get the treatment necessary to assist in healing and you run the risk of creating more damage than you originally started with.

FORGIVENESS MYTH 4: Forgiveness takes time

I've heard it said that "time heals all wounds" but I believe *forgiveness* heals all wounds. Like every other choice in life, we can choose to forgive quickly or slowly. I was reminded of this again when reading about the school shooting that took place in the Amish community in Pennsylvania, USA.

Ten young girls were barricaded in a country schoolhouse and all shot at point-blank range. Sadly five of the girls died at the scene and the other five suffered permanent damage from their horrific injuries. Literally within hours of this shocking tragedy, the Amish community stunned the world by expressing their forgiveness towards the shooter, Charles Carl Roberts IV. They even set up a fund for his wife and children who were left devastated by the events!

Did this forgiveness mean that the Amish community weren't suffering or hurting at the time? Did it mean they weren't experiencing a wide range of emotions? Of course not!

Any person who has experienced loss will go through grief, sorrow, anger, confusion and despair. These emotions are a natural part of the healing process but the reality is this - you don't have to complete the process in order to choose forgiveness! In fact, choosing forgiveness will help *speed up* the healing process.

Regardless of what you have been through in life and regardless of how deeply wounded you have been it *is* possible to make the decision to forgive. Remember - forgiveness is not about feelings! It's a choice that needs to be made in order for healing to take place.

Forgiveness will help the wound that once bled and caused pain, develop layers of new tissue and begin to heal. As time passes a scar will be all that remains. The scar will always serve as a reminder of the injury once sustained but it will no longer cause you pain or suffering.

Forgiveness has helped me see my scars as symbols of recovery, signs of victory and marks of triumph. Instead of living with the pain of my past, forgiveness has allowed me to enjoy my future. These scars are a powerful reminder that even though I was once desperately hurt and wounded, I am now healed and whole! Psalm 30:10 says, *"You turned my wailing into dancing; you removed my sackcloth and clothed me with joy; that my heart may sing to you and not be silent. O Lord my God, I will give you thanks forever."*

Questions to reflect on:

1   What images come to mind when you think about forgiveness? (eg: water rolling off a duck's back, erasing something from a blackboard.)

2   "The weak can never forgive, forgiveness is the attribute of the strong." Do you agree or disagree with this statement and why?

3   How quickly do you embrace forgiveness and what impact does this have on your life and on the lives of those around you?

4   Reflect on a time in your life when you have either forgiven or been forgiven. What was the outcome and how did it make you feel?

5   From what you've read, what daily actions can you take that will help you walk in forgiveness?

KNOW YOUR VALUE

CHAPTER TWELVE - NEW IDENTITY

"There is nothing in a caterpillar that tells you it's going to be a butterfly" - Buckminster Fuller

After I made the decision to become a Christian, God showed me a passage of scripture that really helped me change the way I viewed myself. I usually found it hard believing all the things that God said about me because of my childhood experiences, but my life was changed forever when I read 2 Corinthians 5:17, *"Therefore, if anyone is in Christ, he is a new creation; the **old** has gone, the **new** has come!"*

Time and time again God clearly illustrates His love for new things through His word. It says in Isaiah 65:17, *"Behold I will create **new** heavens and a **new** earth",* and in Ezekiel 36:26, *"I will give you a **new** heart and put a **new** spirit in you."* In the New Testament we read about a **new** covenant, a **new** commandment and a **new** and living way. In case we still fail to believe that God loves making things new He also gave people **new** names to remind them of the change that had taken place in their life. Saul became Paul, Abram became Abraham, Sarai became Sarah and Jacob became Israel.

All of these name changes came after a personal encounter with God and this new name helped them see themselves differently. Every time they were reminded of their past, their new name helped remind them of their future. God is no different today. He is longing to have an encounter with you that will bring about a permanent change not only to your circumstances but how you see yourself!

You might not feel that you are worthy of being given a fresh start, a clean slate or a new identity. And to be honest, in your own strengths and abilities you're not. That is why in Ephesians 2:8-9 it says we are saved by *grace*. Grace is the unmerited favour of God. In other words, even though we were sinners, deserving of judgment, God looked upon us in *love* **and** *forgave* us!

As soon as you accept Christ, God immediately sees you through His eyes. Isaiah 1:18 says, *"Though your sins are like scarlet, they shall be as white as snow; though they are red as crimson, they shall be like wool."* In Christ you are completely clean and perfect. This is your new identity: a perfect child of God. There are no exceptions. The Bible says that God doesn't play favourites - what He promises to one He will deliver to all!

While God promises to give us this new life, it's important that we don't fall into the trap of misinterpreting this promise as an invitation to kick back and expect God to do everything for us. Sadly, too many people think that once they become a Christian, God will wave his magical wand and make everything better, but I've learned that God doesn't work that way. Instead of doing everything for you, He equips you with the tools you need and leaves it up to you to use them!

I believe with all of my heart that the *desire* I had to be liberated from my pain and the choice I made to see myself as a new creation played a huge part in the freedom that I enjoy today.

Instead of constantly allowing my thoughts to remind me of the old me, I chose to see myself as new. Learning to replace these old thoughts with *God's* truth remains one of the most effective and rewarding ways I have learned to deal with my past and it is something that I continue to do on a regular basis. Every time I think about something that gets me down, I turn to God's Word and allow Him to pick me up.

The Apostle Paul says in 2 Corinthians 10:5, *"We demolish arguments and every pretension that sets itself up against the knowledge of God, and **we take captive every thought** to make it obedient to Christ."* If you want to experience the same freedom and walk in the destiny that God has for you, you will have to learn to do the same.

Taking control of your thought life is one of the most important things you can do! Thoughts are like taxis; they have the ability to take you places – good and bad. Regardless of who you are, what you've done and what your personal beliefs are - bringing your thoughts into line with God's Word and replacing lies with truth will result in God's favour and blessing being poured out on your life.

There are three practical steps you need to take in order to do this:

STEP 1 - Identify the negative, repetitive thoughts that you have about yourself or your circumstance, and if it helps, write them down in a journal.

STEP 2 - Find God's truth in the Bible that counteracts the lie that you believe.

STEP 3 - The most important thing is to *believe* God's truth instead of believing the lie.

Here are a few examples of the daily thoughts that I struggled with:

"I'll be tormented by my past forever", but the Bible says, *"if the Son (Jesus) sets you free, you will be free indeed."* John 8:36

"I didn't do well at school therefore I'm not good or smart enough", but the Bible says, *"My grace is sufficient for you, for my power is made perfect in weakness."* 2 Corinthians 12:9

"I'm a victim and will never overcome my past", but the Bible says, *"No, in **all these** things we are more than conquerors through him who loved us."* Romans 8:37

If you find it easier to believe the lies from the Devil than you do believing God's truth, now is the time to do some re-programming. Take out the "CD" that is programmed to play songs of negativity, doubt and stress and start listening to God's truth, which will bring joy, liberty and freedom.

If you don't do this, then the problems of your past will continue to define who you are today! Dwelling on these lies is like having a wound that is trying to heal over but your constant attention and picking at the scab is preventing its full recovery and healing.

Hebrews 12:1 says, *"...let us throw off everything that hinders and the sin that so easily entangles, and let us run with perseverance the race marked out for us!"*

Carrying burdens and negative thoughts around will eventually weigh you down to the point where your life is at a complete standstill. It's the equivalent of running a marathon in searing heat with a fur coat on. Not only is it ineffective, it will prevent you from winning your race and can also make you ill!

It's time to run the race wisely. What is it that hinders you? Is it low self-esteem, a failed marriage, a fear of being unloved or feeling unlovable? Whatever it is that is weighing you down and throwing you off course, it's time to get back on track. It's **never** too late. It's time to see yourself the way Christ sees you – as a new creation!

Here's a great story I read a few years ago that really helped me understand the process of becoming new.

"A man found a cocoon of a butterfly. One day a small opening appeared. He sat and watched the butterfly for several hours as it struggled to force its body through that little hole. Then it seemed to stop making any progress. It appeared as if it had got as far as it could and could go no further. So the man decided to help the butterfly. He took a pair of scissors and snipped off the remaining bit of cocoon. The butterfly then emerged easily, but it had a swollen body and small, shrivelled wings.

The man continued to watch the butterfly because he expected that at any moment the wings would enlarge and expand to be able to support the body, which would contract in time. Neither happened! In fact, the butterfly spent the rest of its life crawling around with a swollen body and shrivelled wings. It never was able to fly.

What the man in his kindness and haste failed to understand was that the restricting cocoon, and the struggle required to break through the tiny opening, were God's way of helping it to fly. You see, the pressure created from going through the opening forced the fluid from the body of the butterfly into its wings, so it would be ready for flight once it achieved its freedom from the cocoon.

Sometimes struggles are exactly what we need in our life. If God allowed us to go through our life without any obstacles, it would cripple us. We would not be as strong as what we could have been, and we would never fly."

We are no different to the butterfly. If we push through the circumstances that contain us and allow them to be used by God, we too will come out the other side stronger and able to soar above the adversity and challenges of life. So keep pushing forward, and once you've experienced your break through - don't look back.

The butterfly doesn't spend the rest of its life dwelling on the fact that it was once bound and nor should you. Christ has come to liberate you and set you free for a reason. Matthew 10:8, *"Freely you have received, freely give."* Don't waste your freedom or the blessings that you've received. Share them with others and be a blessing!

CHAPTER THIRTEEN — SHAME*LESS*

"Everyone needs a sense of shame, but no one needs to feel ashamed." - Frederick Nietzschese

One month after my 22nd birthday, I had the privilege of bringing our beautiful daughter Kealy Jai into the world. She was without a doubt the most adorable baby that I had ever laid eyes on and Ross and I were both absolutely besotted with her arrival into our lives.

Like all first time parents, Ross and I had to adapt our lifestyle and make changes that would accommodate our new arrival. While we felt somewhat prepared for these changes and anticipated the sleepless nights and extra costs that went hand-in-hand with parenthood, there was one change I wasn't prepared for; and that was fear.

I suddenly became fearful of everything that related to parenting; including things that could go wrong now as well as the things that might go wrong in the future. I worried about everything from not having enough milk for breastfeeding to cot death and everything else in-between. I also worried about my ability to protect her from things outside of my control. I remember thinking to myself that if my parents couldn't protect me from being abused, what makes me think I could protect Kealy? It was because of this that I felt completely overwhelmed with the responsibility of raising a child and felt desperately inadequate.

Experiencing this overwhelming fear triggered a whole host of different emotions within me. I began to realise that this fear was deeply rooted in shame, guilt, insecurity, inferiority and inadequacy that stemmed from my childhood experiences. Even though I had been a Christian now for over three years I realised that I still had a long road to walk till my healing was complete.

It's amazing how God uses our memories to help us deal with the root issues in our past. Up until Kealy was born, I had suppressed the memories of the abuse and had buried them deep in the recesses of my mind. Yet it was becoming more obvious that while I had suppressed these memories, they were still affecting my life.

I started to realise that the shame and guilt from my abuse were major contributing factors in some of the issues I still faced. On top of feeling inadequate and fearful, I had particular issues in the area of intimacy. I didn't have a problem being "touchy feely" with friends and family, in fact, I was often the first one to reach out for a hug or a kiss. But when it came to intimacy in marriage, I struggled a lot.

Whenever Ross wanted to hug me or show me affection of any kind, I would often push him away and make out that I didn't have time. He would often get upset with this apparent rejection and while he was left hurt, I was left annoyed and frustrated that my past still had control of this area of my life.

The abuse that I endured as a child not only robbed me of my innocence, self-esteem and value, but also of the ability to trust others - including my husband who I loved dearly. Instead of seeing his signs of affection as something to be enjoyed, I saw them as something to be mistrusted and wary of.

I knew that it was time to confront these issues head on so I could be free to live my life to the full. If I didn't, I knew things would only get worse. While I was aware that dealing with these issues would be difficult, I also knew the way to do this successfully was to invite God into the areas of my life that were broken.

There were two specific things that God showed me during this time and both of them played a significant role in helping free me from my shame.

The first one was confession:

1 John 1:9 says, *"If we confess our sins (shortfalls), he is faithful and just and will forgive us our sins and* **purify** *us from all unrighteousness."* I knew that once I exposed these feelings of shame through confession, God would help liberate me from it.

Confession allows God to forgive us and it also purifies us from our wrongful deeds, unlike denial, which does the opposite. Denial binds us up and prevents us from experiencing healing and freedom. After all, if you can't admit that you have a problem in your life, it's obvious you can't get the help needed to make the problem go away!

Ephesians 5:8 says this, *"For you were once in darkness, but now you are light in the Lord."*

I believe the enemy, the devil, operates in darkness and secrecy. If you are carrying around deep dark secrets that you're too ashamed or embarrassed to tell anyone about, the enemy has you exactly where he wants you! You need to expose those things and bring them out of the darkness and into light. Confessing and exposing your need will give God an opportunity to meet it. It will help set you free from the very thing that once kept your heart heavy and your eyes downcast.

The second thing was looking to God and training my mind on this issue. Some of the verses I meditated on to renew my mind and to believe the right things were:

Psalm 34:4-5 says, *"I sought the Lord, and he answered me; he delivered me from all my fears. Those who look to him are radiant; their faces are never covered with shame."*

Isaiah 61:7 *"Instead of their shame my people will receive a double portion, and instead of disgrace they will rejoice in their inheritance; and so they will inherit a double portion in their land, and everlasting joy will be theirs."*

Job 11:13 *"Yet if you devote your heart to him and stretch out your hands to him, if you put away the sin that is in your hand and allow no evil to dwell in your tent, then you will lift up your face without shame; you will stand firm and without fear."*

Psalm 3:3 *"...you bestow glory on me and lift up my head...."*

Isaiah 57:18 *"I have seen his ways, but I will heal him; I will guide him and restore comfort to him".*

As I meditated on these scriptures, I noticed that the cloud of shame that once overshadowed areas of my life slowly started to dissipate. The healing process had begun its work and I was finding my sense of value, self-worth, as well as the ability to trust again, being restored.

Years after the abuse had stopped, I started to feel God urging me to confront my abuser. People in the past had suggested I do this, if possible, but at first I was completely closed off to the idea. I just didn't feel there was a need to drag up the past, especially considering I was now happily married, well adjusted, healed and whole. But the more I told myself it was unnecessary, the more I felt God urge me to do it.

After much thought and deliberation I finally decided that if God wanted this to happen then I would have a willing and open heart. In 1 Samuel 15:22 it says, *"To obey is better than sacrifice..."* While obeying God can sometimes be difficult to do, I've learned that there is absolutely no denying the benefits.

While I was happy with the fact that I was now *prepared* to confront my abuser, never in my wildest dreams did I think it would actually happen. After all, twenty years had passed since the abuse had taken place!

A couple of years later however, an opportunity that can only be described as divinely orchestrated presented itself. While I was absolutely convinced that God had arranged this meeting, I was still filled with fear and anxiety over addressing the issue. In the moments immediately beforehand I had a million questions running through my mind. "Would he deny the abuse happened or somehow justify it? Would he try and shift the blame on to me and say it was my fault? Would he admit that what he did was wrong and take full responsibility for it?"

There was only one way to find out.

As I started talking to him I was relieved that his response was the latter. He made no excuses for the decisions he had made and expressed sorrow and regret for what had happened. Because our meeting was unexpected, we didn't have long to talk, but as the conversation drew to a close I felt an incredible weight lift off my shoulders.

I felt relieved that he showed remorse for what had happened and that he appeared to have moved on with his life. But more importantly, I was relieved by the fact that I had finally been given the opportunity to talk to him about God's amazing ability to heal, restore and forgive!

I wasn't interested in telling him how much he had hurt me or how much the abuse affected my life. I was far more interested in letting him know that the power of God can transform any life, regardless of how damaged or broken and in spite of the mistakes made.

When I think back to this incredible time I am so grateful that I didn't close the door on this God-given opportunity. I may never find out if the things I shared that day changed his life, but at least I got the chance to tell him how much God had changed *my* life.

CHAPTER FOURTEEN
YOU ARE PRICELESS

"Every individual has a place to fill in the world and is important in some respect, whether he chooses to be so or not!" - Nathanial Hawthorne

For the majority of my teenage years I lived a double life. During the day, surrounded with friends, I came across as a fun loving, outgoing and a happy-go-lucky kind of girl. But locked away in the privacy of my bedroom, I was riddled with inadequacy, insecurity and feelings of never measuring up.

Nothing I did felt right or good enough and I started to believe that even doing well was a waste of time. Before long I placed no value on my life or on anything I did.

As the years have gone by and I've reflected on my past, the more aware I've become of the different ways that feelings of inadequacy, insecurity and unworthiness can unveil themselves.

Some people like me, completely give up on themselves and get lost in a world of hopelessness and despair. They say to themselves that no matter how hard they try, regardless of how good they are, or how well they do, it makes little or no difference to the outcome of their life. They sadly believe that this is their lot in life and their world remains warped and distorted by the view that they have of themselves and their circumstances.

There are also people who deal with their feelings of inadequacy in the opposite way. They fall into the trap of *striving* in order to obtain value and worth. These people are often high achievers but sadly they depend on these accomplishments to gain significance, importance and value. While these accomplishments will often gain the praises of people and be enjoyed for a time, it never satisfies the need they have to be loved and accepted for who they are!

Regardless of whether you're a high achiever or a failure in your own eyes – in the eyes of God you're valued and worthy!

Deuteronomy 7:6 says, *"For you are a people holy to the Lord your God. The Lord your God has chosen you out of all the peoples on the face of the earth to be his people, his* **treasured possession.***"*

God places such value on you because He loves you! You are His creation, His masterpiece. You are His child. You might not feel lovable or valuable because of bad decisions or unfortunate circumstances but your value isn't measured by the mistakes you've made or the decisions you regret. You're value simply comes from being part of God's creation!

Psalm 139:13-16 says, *"For you created my inmost being; you knit me together in my mother's womb. I praise you because I am fearfully and wonderfully made; your works are wonderful, I know that full well. My frame was not hidden from you when I was made in the secret place. When I was woven together in the depths of the earth, your eyes saw my unformed body. All the days ordained for me were written in your book before one of them came to be."*

If you struggle believing you are valuable because of the things you've done wrong, think of it this way - does the value of a coin ever change? Does a coin become less valuable because a drug-pusher or a rapist has handled it? Is it devalued by years of wear and tear? The answer of course is no! The value of the coin is pre-determined.

Jesus told the parables of the lost coin, the lost sheep and the lost son. Through these stories Jesus is communicating the value he places on us, and the extreme lengths he goes to, to save us. I remember years ago hearing the story of my mother-in-law who lost her brand new denture in an outback pit toilet. Even though the denture was lost in a pit of sewage, the value of the denture drove her to find it again. (You'll be pleased to know it was sterilised several times before being re-used!) The lesson here is this. The more you value something, the more desperate you become to find it if it becomes lost!

You are no different. Jesus Christ loves you *so* much and places such value on you that He was willing to pay the highest price to bring you back into a relationship with Him. He paid with His own life. He knew the agony that lay ahead and the humiliation He was to endure, He knew the taunting that was to come, and yet in spite of all the suffering, He counted the cost and said, "You are worth it all!"

Why don't you take a few moments to really stop and think about that? Jesus Christ went to the cross and died because He knew it would bridge the gap that sin had created between man and God. He knew this bridge would bring freedom to a world full of hurting people; He knew it would bring freedom to you! It would provide a way for you to be healed physically, emotionally and spiritually and would help you live a life full of love, joy and peace instead of a life bound with depression, sorrow and anger.

This sacrifice is the greatest expression of God's love the world has ever seen, but still many people struggle to accept that God really loves and values them.

I can certainly appreciate that there are times when we *feel* devalued. Like me, you may have been abused when you were young. You may have grown up only ever hearing negative feedback or been abandoned or rejected; but the fact of the matter is this - just because you *feel* devalued doesn't mean you *are* devalued! Remember: feelings can't always be trusted, but God's promises can be!

There are almost one hundred references in the New Testament that refer to the promises that we have in Christ.
2 Corinthians 1:20 says, *"For no matter how many promises God has made, they are 'Yes' in Christ!"* It is through Jesus Christ that all God's promises of good things are accessible, regardless of what you have been through!

When we devalue ourselves it becomes difficult to lay hold of the promises that are available to us. The Bible says that in Christ we have:

- A new start (2 Corinthians 5:17)
- Peace (Philippians 4:7)
- Provision (Philippians 4:19)
- Freedom from condemnation (Romans 8:1)
- Equality (Galatians 3:28)
- Victory (2 Corinthians 2:14)

When we choose to see ourselves the way that Christ sees us, the easier it becomes to overcome the obstacles that come against us in life.

The Apostle Paul is a great biblical example of a person who chose to see himself "in Christ" despite making some poor choices in life and enduring much adversity! The book of Acts tells us a bit about Paul prior to his conversion and how he murdered and tormented Christians. In Acts 9:13 a man named Ananias says, *"I have heard many reports about this man and all the harm he has done to your saints in Jerusalem."*

In the book of 1 Timothy, Paul recognised his past mistakes and the error of his ways, which included murdering and torturing Christians, and referred to himself as the *"worst of sinners."* Yet despite these mistakes, Paul refused to let them drag him down or define his future. He chose to see himself the way God did: loved, chosen and respected. He simply drew a line in the sand and chose to see himself in Christ.

I love how he starts his letter to the church in Rome. It says: *"**Paul, a servant** of Christ Jesus, **called** to be an apostle and set apart for the gospel of God."* Paul not only chose to embrace his new identity, he also understood that God had created him for a purpose. He knew that he was called to be an apostle and that no trial or tribulation was going to distract him from that. Paul had his eyes fixed on the plans and purposes that God had prepared for him.

We should do exactly the same. Don't let past experiences or problems prevent you from embracing all that God has prepared for you! Don't allow yourself to get bitter because adversity has come your way or because your plans haven't gone the way you had hoped.

Isaiah 54:17 says, *"no weapon formed against you will prevail"* and Proverbs 19:21, *"many are the plans in a man's heart, but it is the Lord's purpose that prevails."* Regardless of the situation or circumstance you face, God loves you and wants to see His purposes come to pass in your life!

Don't allow the enemy to deceive you into thinking that God can't use you because of what you've been through. God doesn't care about past mistakes or failures and neither does He think you're less valuable because of them! God will never place you on the discount rack because you have been broken, mistreated or abused. He paid the **full price** for you on the cross two thousand years ago because He knew that absolutely NOTHING could ever decrease your value!

If you are feeling devalued, lost or broken, God *can* and *will* still use you! There are countless stories of God using people that were deemed unworthy either by themselves or by people around them. Moses, Gideon, Esther, and Peter are just a few of the many biblical names that could be mentioned.

King David is another man who was broken after he had sinned against God. He not only committed adultery but also had the woman's husband murdered to cover up her resulting pregnancy. In Psalm 51:17 David says, *"...a broken and a contrite heart, O God, you will not despise."* Despite

David's brokenness and his many mistakes, he is known throughout history as a man after God's own heart.

We might despise our own brokenness but God does not! In fact, I believe He places value on it! Matthew 5:3 says, *"Blessed are the poor in spirit, for theirs is the kingdom of heaven."*

The challenge for us is this - don't despise your brokenness! Hand it over to God and allow Him to use it for the extension of His kingdom. Instead of allowing your circumstances to devalue you, let them qualify you. Allow God to use the things you've been through to help others.

I honestly believe if we spend *less* time thinking about the things we've done wrong or what makes us *feel* devalued and spend more time focusing on what *Christ* did on the cross for us, then we would truly appreciate how priceless we truly are.

Remember: despite how we see ourselves or how others see us, Jesus Christ loves us and places value on us!

Questions to reflect on:

1   If you could change one thing about yourself, what would it be and why?

2   What is your biggest fear in life and why do you think that is?

3   If you struggle with low self-esteem, what/who do you feel triggers it and why?

4   Having high self-esteem means that you value yourself. What are the things you value most about yourself?

5a)   Make a list of negative beliefs you have about yourself. Where do those negative beliefs come from?

 b) Write down God's truths that counteract these negative beliefs?

WINNING PRINCIPLES

CHAPTER FIFTEEN - WEB OR WONDER?

"The pessimist sees difficulty in every opportunity.
The optimist sees the opportunity in every difficulty"
- Winston Churchill

It might be difficult to imagine that anything positive could come out of the tragedy that our family endured. However Romans 8:28 says: *"...in all things God works for the good of those who love him, who have been called according to his purposes."*

You might feel that your circumstance is outside of God's reach or control but the fact is everything you've been through can be turned around to benefit you and those around you. That means every struggle, every situation, and every sacrifice - absolutely everything!

Not only does God promise to work everything out for our good, but in James 1:2 the apostle Paul urges the church to, *"Consider it pure joy, my brothers, when you face trials of many kinds..."* How can Paul have such a positive outlook on life? The answer is this: he saw things from God's perspective! In verses two and three of the same passage, Paul goes onto explain why: *"**because** you know that the testing of your faith develops perseverance. Perseverance must finish its work so that **you** may be mature and complete, **not lacking anything!"***

Paul didn't rejoice because of the trial itself but because of what the trial would produce in his life. I remember being in labour with Kealy and the excruciating pain that I endured for almost thirteen hours. I can't honestly say that I rejoiced during my labour experience, but I did rejoice knowing that after my labour, I was going to hold my precious and beautiful baby.

Life is all about perspective. Can you believe that your trial or the challenges you face have the ability to produce something beautiful in your life?

I believe you can see the situation you face in two ways. Like a tapestry, you can view it from the front and appreciate the beauty of the picture before you. Or you can stand behind the tapestry where you will only see the messy web of knots, threads and loose ends. From this perspective life looks messy, ugly and has no order or purpose.

However, the creator of the tapestry sees it in its entirety. She understands that if there were no knotted mess and interwoven strands of thread going every which way on the back, there would be no tapestry for people to admire on the front.

We need to see our life from *God's* viewpoint. We need to stand at the front of the artwork and appreciate its beauty while at the same time valuing the process by which it was made. Instead of viewing the messy knots negatively, begin to appreciate them and realise that it is during these times of difficulty that beauty is created.

For a long time I struggled coming to terms with my past. I hated being reminded of the things that had taken place in my life not only because it was painful dwelling on it but also because I was embarrassed and ashamed. In fact it took me about ten years of walking with God before I got to a place where I began to truly appreciate my past and understood that it was during those dark times that a lot of my passion was formed.

Because I have experienced pain and suffering, I am now passionate about seeing people set free from those things. I am passionate about offering hope because I know what it is like to not have it. I am passionate about being available for young people because I know what can happen when young people feel they don't have anyone to turn to.

Maybe it's a strange way of seeing it, but your experiences qualify you to teach others. What is in your past that could be turned around for good? Are you passionate about preventing child abuse, domestic violence, drug and alcohol abuse or prostitution? Why not use the things that have hurt you to give you purpose, meaning and help make a difference in somebody else's life.

The incredible thing about living life this way is that instead of trying to forget your past, God will help you *use* it! He will use your experiences and mistakes, and draw out valuable lessons that will enable you to help others. God will give you His perspective on life!

A number of years ago I was flying over Greenland on a flight to Nashville, USA. A few hours had passed when the pilot announced that we would soon see some icebergs in the ocean below. As they came into view, the beauty of what I saw took my breath away; but the thing that struck me the most was how *small* the icebergs seemed to be from 10,000ft in the air! I was reminded that this is how God wants us to view our problems. When we have God's perspective, our problems appear to be much smaller than what they are in reality.

Human nature has a tendency to go into crisis mode and to think about the worst case scenario when things don't go according to plan. We allow our minds to think of all the potential problems instead of the potential provision; we think of the opposition instead of the opportunity and we live in fear instead of faith.

In Colossians 3:1 Paul says, *"Set your minds on things above, not on earthly things."*

Why don't you ask God to help you see each trial and season of difficulty from His perspective? Then take the next step and allow Him to use it for your good and for the good of those around you!

CHAPTER SIXTEEN - WHAT'S YOUR FREQUENCY?

"Listen to my instruction and be wise; do not ignore it. Blessed is the man who listens to me...and receives favour from the Lord." Proverbs 8:33-35

When Kealy was just a few months old, feeling discontented and frustrated with life, I allowed myself to tune in and listen to the wrong voices. Ross and I had been married for a couple of years and had relocated due to a promotion at his work. Though this was a fantastic opportunity for Ross, it meant that we had to move almost an hour away from our family, friends and church. Although we still saw them on the weekends, living away from home made me feel isolated, trapped and disconnected from my support network.

During this difficult time of transition I started spending a lot of time with an ex-boyfriend from school. While I knew it probably wasn't the wisest thing to be doing, it felt much better than being on my own. Peter was in-between jobs at this time and though he was looking for something permanent he had a lot of spare time on his hands.

Even though our relationship had long since ended, we had remained pretty close friends. This was made particularly easy by the fact that we were now both committed Christians and attending the same church.

Initially I was blinded by the temptation and we continued spending more and more time together. It wasn't too long before people in church started commenting on how inappropriate it was for us to be spending so much time together and started making suggestions that we stop. I can clearly remember the feelings of indignation. Who did they think they were? I was a grown adult and if I wanted to hang out with an old friend, then I would. The more people said it was wrong, the more offended I became and instead of heeding their Godly advice, I defended my actions.

A few months later, I became increasingly aware that my feelings of friendship towards Peter had grown and I knew that there was more to this relationship than I had previously been willing to acknowledge.

I had convinced myself that there was nothing wrong with the feelings we had for each other. I had stopped tuning into the voice of Godly counsel and wisdom and started listening to lies and deceit.

So deceived was I, that at one point I actually started to believe that I would be happier with Peter than I would with Ross! It took me twelve months of heartache and confusion before I finally invited God into the situation. From past experience I knew that God was well able to turn this potentially devastating circumstance around. All He needed was for me to start listening to His voice and obey Him.

Years later I still can't believe how naive I was for allowing things to spiral out of control as much as they did. Thankfully, I finally realised the deception I was in and started listening to the right voices again. I almost lost everything because of this costly mistake.

After repenting and confessing the error of my ways and with the wonderful support of our senior pastors and families, Ross and I overcame the odds and went from strength to strength. In spite of it all, Ross remained completely faithful to God and though there were times when he heard the voices of negativity and doubt, he ultimately chose to tune in and listen to what God was saying.

When I think back to this time I can see very clearly the plans of the enemy to strip me of everything that I held dear. It is amazingly easy to tune into the voices of frustration, disappointment and discontentment with quite devastating consequences, instead of tuning in to God and allowing *His* voice to lead and guide us.

In western culture we are constantly bombarded with voices that tell us if we do this or buy that we will be happy, successful and fulfilled. We need to seriously wise up and recognise that not every voice we listen to is a good voice. While this seems blatantly obvious, it's amazing how many people fall for these lies and deceptions.

Countless babies are being aborted, husbands are leaving wives, wives are leaving husbands, addictions are taking control and depression and anxiety are continually on the rise. People's lives all over the world are being destroyed because people are tuning into the wrong frequency.

1 Peter 5:8 tells us, *"Be self-controlled and alert. Your enemy the devil prowls around like a roaring lion looking for* **someone to devour.** *Resist him, standing firm in the faith...."*

In Matthew 4 we read how Jesus was tempted by the voice of Satan in His time of weakness. Note: it is usually during a moment of weakness that Satan will come and tempt you. After spending forty days and forty nights fasting in the wilderness, the enemy came and tried to tempt Jesus with power, wealth, pleasure and fame.

How did Jesus resist these temptations? What was the secret to His success? The answer is very simple. He knew which voice to listen to. Once He identified the voice of the enemy, He retaliated with the Word of God. We need to do the same!

You may have faced times of temptation in the past too; a little lie here, a compromise there. Before you know it, you're entertaining the voice of the enemy instead of rebuking it! Don't allow the voice of the enemy to deceive and rob you of all that God has planned for you. Know what God's Word says. Trust Him, be patient and don't act in haste!

In the book of John, Jesus actually refers to himself as "the good shepherd." The responsibility of a shepherd is to take care of sheep and to ensure they are protected from all kinds of harm. Just like a shepherd tends to sheep in the natural realm, Jesus is our shepherd in the spiritual.

Jesus Christ loves you and wants to see you prospering and blessed in every area of your life, but He also wants to protect you from the pitfalls and hazards that come across your path. In order for this to happen, you have to listen for His guidance and be obedient to His instruction. If you're unsure of what to do, you need to find out what the Bible says about your situation or circumstance.

John 10:4 says, "...his sheep follow him because they know his voice. But they will never follow a stranger; in fact, they will run away from him because they do not recognise a stranger's voice." Are you tuned in to the shepherd's frequency?

Resisting temptation and tuning to God's frequency is not as hard as you think. You simply need to tune out of the other frequencies and obey God's Word. James 4:7 says, *"Submit yourselves, then, to God.* **Resist** *the devil, and he will* **flee** *from you. Come near to God and he will come near to you."*

It also says in 1 Corinthians 10:13, *"God is faithful; he will not let you be tempted beyond what you can bear. But when you are tempted, he will also provide a way out so that you can stand up under it!"*

It's always important to draw close to God, but it's even more crucial in times of doubt, confusion and uncertainty. Just like the wolf that picks off the sick and vulnerable sheep on the fringe of the herd, the enemy is looking to pick off people who are in times of difficulty and feeling vulnerable.

So...are you tuned into God's frequency or someone else's? Who are you allowing to lead and guide you? If you recognise that you are being led astray by the "strangers" voice, now is the time to draw a line in the sand and start over. It's time to start afresh and allow yourself to be led by the one who loves and cares for you – Jesus Christ, the true Shepherd.

CHAPTER SEVENTEEN - A GRATEFUL HEART

"He is a wise man who does not grieve for the things which he has not, but rejoices for those which he has." - Epicetus

Despite the dramatic turnaround in my life, there were still times when I struggled with anger, resentment and negativity.

Christmas Day was without a doubt one of the most difficult times for me. Instead of being able to enjoy quality time with my family like other people, I was reminded of the tensions that ran deep in our family and of the ongoing impact the tragedies had on my life.

With my brothers no longer having contact with each other, aunts and uncles falling out with Mum and me trying to see everyone and keeping everyone happy, I was often left feeling emotionally and physically exhausted by the end of Christmas day. This exhaustion often meant that I would over-react to even the simplest of things. I remember one time having a major argument with Ross because I asked him if the dress I was wearing needed to be ironed, to which he said no. But then when we were out, he said "actually, it could have done with an ironing!" I was absolutely furious with him!

There have been countless other times over the years when I've had to battle these feelings of resentment and anger. Common triggers included the anniversary of the attacks, Father's Day or watching TV when images of death and violence appear. At times even happy occasions like going to weddings and listening to people talk about their childhood experiences could set me off on an emotional rollercoaster.

As time went by I began to realise that even though many years had come and gone since the traumatic events of my youth, the impact they continued to have on my life was still significant. One of the areas that suffered the most was in my marriage.

More specifically, it was the way I dealt with conflict within our marriage. When arguments broke out between us, which thankfully weren't too often, I could literally feel a "tidal wave" of anger rising within me. Not knowing how to deal with this powerful emotion, I allowed it to gain momentum until it came crashing down, wreaking havoc on our lives. Cutting words or physical violence left Ross feeling confused and hurt, while I felt ashamed and scared by my appalling behaviour.

Seeing the devastating impact these emotional outbursts had on my life caused me to start getting real about the issues I faced. The realisation came that unless I learned to deal with these unresolved emotions, my past would always play a role in my future; ultimately robbing me of the life that God had created me to live.

This desire to be free from my emotional baggage caused me to look closer at my life and try and identify the things that triggered these emotional outbursts. As I started to do this, I noticed two patterns unfold.

First of all, almost every major episode or outburst of anger was triggered because I had recently been dwelling on the losses in my life. The more I focused on these, the more I justified the outbursts of anger. While many would say it was understandable, I knew it was stopping me from living life to the full.

The other pattern I noticed was the more I thought about and focused on the things I was really thankful for, the happier and calmer I felt. Instead of carrying the weight of the world on my shoulders, I found I had a smile on my face and a skip in my step.

It says in Philippians 4:8-9, *"Finally, brothers, whatever is true, whatever is noble, whatever is right, whatever is pure, whatever is lovely, whatever is admirable – if anything is excellent or praiseworthy – think about such things…And the God of peace will be with you. "*

Identifying these two patterns and the different outcomes they produced in my life made me realise the importance of really developing and honing this attitude of thanksgiving.

I believe wholeheartedly that everyone has the ability to cultivate gratitude, regardless of the circumstances. Just start by being thankful for the things you *have* in life, instead of dwelling on what you *don't* have. You might not think that you have much in life to be thankful for and like me you might have been through horrific circumstances; but I challenge you to stop justifying your emotions and feeling sorry for yourself! Regardless of what you have been through in life there is *always* something to be thankful for.

You might be the type of person who takes for granted the blessings in your world because of familiarity and complacency. Instead of appreciating your family or your job, you complain about the responsibility and busyness that they generate. It's not until you hear of someone else's tragedy or loss that you are reminded of how truly blessed you are to have these things in your world.

Having experienced personal tragedy at a young age I grew up with a deep understanding of how fragile life can be.

This awareness has helped me to appreciate the small things in life and made it easier to avoid the complacency trap.

Here are just a few of the things that I regularly give thanks for:

- My relationship with God and His guidance.
- Ross and the amazing relationship we have.
- My kids and the joy they bring to my life.
- Friends who challenge and inspire me.
- A loving relationship with my family
- A loving relationship with Ross' family
- A job that fulfils me.
- Friends who have fun and make me laugh.
- Good health for my family and I.
- My church family.
- Technology and for things that make my life easier.
- A roof over my head and food on the table.

There's more but I have to stop somewhere!

What are some of the things that have blessed your life? Do you take them for granted? Why don't you take a few moments to think about these things? Jot them down on a piece of paper and put them up in a place where you can see them regularly. Each day spend some time thinking about them and expressing thanks for them. I guarantee that if you do this on a regular basis, you will begin to notice a difference in your attitude and approach to life!

If you struggle thinking of things to be thankful for, try thinking about what life would be like *without* certain things. Think about life without running water or electricity, food or transport, TV or music. Take a few moments and think about the thousands of victims of the 2004 Tsunami. I'm not just talking about the ones who lost their lives but the ones who lost their husbands, wives, children, homes, possessions, security and peace of mind. It's a sad but true fact, that most people don't really appreciate what they have in life, until there's a possibility that it could be taken away from them!

The apostle Paul is a great biblical example of someone who endured many hardships and experienced great loss and yet still managed to be thankful for the things that he had in life. Almost every letter he wrote to the churches in the New Testament begins with an expression of thanksgiving; yet he endured so much.

2 Corinthians 11:23 says, *"I have worked much harder, been in prison more frequently, been flogged more severely, and been exposed to death again and again. Five times I received from the Jews the forty lashes minus one. Three times I was beaten with rods, once I was stoned, three times I was shipwrecked, I spent a night and a day in the open sea, I have been constantly on the move. I have been in danger from rivers, in danger from bandits, in danger from my own countrymen, in danger from Gentiles; in danger in the city, in danger in the country, in danger at sea; and in danger from false brothers. I have laboured and toiled and have often gone without sleep; I have known hunger and thirst and have often*

gone without food; I have been cold and naked. Besides everything else, I face daily the pressure of my concern for all the churches."

I don't know what challenges you're facing in life, but I'm sure they're not as difficult as Paul's circumstances! While he could be excused for curling up into the foetal position and giving up, he pressed on and overcame!

Philippians 4:11, *"...for I have learned to be content **whatever** the circumstances. I know what it is to be in need and I know what it is to have plenty. I have learned the secret of being content in **any** and **every** situation..."*

I remember reading this scripture many years ago and literally feeling hope rise within me! Paul's life provided me with a real life example of someone who had experienced hardships but had learned to rise above them; if Paul could learn to be content despite everything he had been through, then I could too!

You might not have everything in life that you want and you might still be waiting for your dreams to unfold. Don't stress out about it and act in haste - just relax and trust God. David tells us in Psalm 37:3, *"**Trust** in the Lord and do good; dwell in the land and enjoy safe pasture. **Delight** yourself in the Lord and he will give you the desires of your heart."* The fact that your prayers have not yet been answered does not mean that they will remain unanswered! Begin thanking God for what you do have, and believe Him for what you're waiting to receive.

Here is a poem I received a number of years ago that really helped me cultivate an attitude of gratitude. I pray that as you read it, you will begin to realise that in every situation there is something to be thankful for!

"Be thankful that you don't have everything you desire;
If you did, what would there be to look forward to?

Be thankful when you don't know something
For it gives you the opportunity to learn.

Be thankful for the difficult times;
During those times you grow.

Be thankful for your limitations;
It will build your strength and character.

Be thankful for your mistakes;
They will teach you valuable lessons.

Be thankful when you're tired and weary;
Because it means you've made a difference

A life of rich fulfilment comes to those who are
also thankful for their setbacks!

GRATITUDE is powerful! It can turn a negative into a positive, so...find a way to be thankful for your troubles and they can become your blessings!"

Questions to reflect on:

1   Are you the type of person who sees difficulty in every opportunity, or the opportunity in every difficulty? Why?

2   How do you respond to the challenges that come against you in life and what impact does this have on you and those around you?

3   Take a few moments to reflect on the things in your life that you are grateful for. Write them down and meditate on them frequently.

4   When was the last time you felt like quitting? What happened and what was the outcome?

5   "Your attitude determines your altitude." Do you agree with this statement and why?

CONCLUSION

I know that God loves you and wants the best for you. He wants to heal you emotionally, spiritually and physically. He wants you to walk into a future that He has planned for you which is filled with promise and hope.

Jeremiah 29:11 says, *"'For I know the plans I have for you', declares the Lord, 'plans to prosper you and not to harm you, plans to give you hope and a future. Then you will call upon me and come and pray to me, and I will listen to you. You will seek me and find me when you seek me with **all** of your heart'."*

Whether you allow God to make these promises a reality in your life or not is entirely up to you! If you choose to put into practice the principles I have outlined in this book then I believe they will be a reality.

It might not be easy! In the book of Philippians the apostle Paul says *"...one thing I do: Forgetting what is behind me and* **straining** *toward what is ahead, I* **press** *on towards the goal to win the prize for which God has called me heavenward in Christ Jesus."*

I love the terminology that Paul uses here! He uses words like "**straining** toward" and "**pressing** on." What he's saying is that it's not always *easy* to break free from the things that once hurt you, but he knows that with perseverance it will pay off. If we keep pressing on, if we keep straining towards the goal, eventually we will obtain the prize that God has prepared for us!

In Matthew 6:33 Jesus says, *"...seek first his kingdom and his righteousness, and all these things will be given to you as well."* So many times I could have allowed the past to distract me and yet because I refuse to give in to my circumstances and keep my eyes firmly fixed on Him, God has proven Himself faithful time and time again!

God is certainly willing and able to do the same in your life; to heal your brokenness, meet your need, restore that which has been stolen and free you from your past. In fact, God is able to do *more* than what you ever-dreamed possible. Ephesians 3:20 says, *"Now to him who is able to do* **immeasurably more** *than all we ask or imagine, according to his power that is at work within us..."*

We all go through seasons in life that stretch and challenge us. Times where it feels like there is a lot of hard work and not always a lot of progress - but don't be tempted to opt out or give up! Don't allow yourself to stay in that place of brokenness and be crippled by your past, just because persevering seems too hard.

I have become so aware over the years that if you want a breakthrough in an area you have to learn to follow through. You have to follow through when the going gets tough and there's a temptation to revert back to your old way of living. You have to follow through when you've been called to walk by faith instead of living in fear! Don't let the fear of failure, fear of uncertainty or the fear of confronting circumstances rob you of the possibilities and opportunities that are readily available in God.

I remember working in a doctor's surgery years ago and being asked to take photos of a massive ulcerating tumour on the side of a woman's face. This tumour was so massive it had its own blood supply and was starting to spread to her mouth, nose and eyes. It was so disfiguring that she had stopped going out in public and at night had to wrap her pillow in towels to absorb the secretions from the tumour! (Nice picture huh?)

When questioned by the doctor why she had taken eighteen months to seek medical help, the answer was shocking. Her response was "fear!" While this story is quite graphic, it provides a very powerful illustration of how debilitating fear can be. If you let it, fear will cripple and rob you of the abundant life that Jesus Christ died on the cross for!

In John 10:10 Jesus says, *"I have come that they may have life and have it to the full"* and Jesus **always** keeps His promises.

While it takes a certain amount of determination and courage to confront issues, the damage that is caused by leaving them to fester and grow is far more costly! The woman in the example above had to undergo hours of facial reconstruction because she failed to confront her fear. This tumour, though it was benign, left her with scars that will last a lifetime despite the fact that it started as a tiny little lump.

I want to encourage you to deal with the lumps in your life! They may seem small now but if left, they will develop into something nasty. Whatever is holding you back in life and preventing you from living the life created by God for you, whatever is keeping you in the darkness and stopping you from shining brightly, I pray that the principles in this book will help you to walk in victory!

Like many of you, I am still on a journey. God hasn't finished with me yet and there are still many things He wants me to learn and grow through; but whilst I go through the process, I can confidently say that God, who began a good work in me, will carry it on to completion!

I pray after having read this book that you can too…

EPILOGUE

Despite suffering multiple stab wounds and having to stay in hospital for a number of months, Mum made a full recovery - though there have been a couple of life threatening complications since then. Thanks to my mum's incredible strength, stamina and resilience, these complications were only momentary setbacks. She continues to live a very full and happy life in Newcastle with Ray her partner of over 20 years. She believes Jesus saved her on the night of the attacks and attends church occasionally. She enjoys a loving relationship with myself, and both of my brothers.

My mum, brothers and their wives are aware that this book has been published, and are happy for our story to be shared.

Sadly the relationship between my aunties, uncles and cousins on my dad's side has never been fully restored. I have on the odd occasion run into them in the street and while it's amicable there's no denying the pain that still exists.

Andrew lives in Queensland, Australia and has recently married his girlfriend of 10 years. They are excited about the arrival of their firstborn due in April 2012. He works in the building industry and is a much-loved member our family.

David is happily married with three beautiful daughters and lives in Brisbane, Australia. After ten years of severing all ties with Andrew he finally chose forgiveness and restored the relationship. They both now see each other on a regular basis.

At the time of writing this, my brothers have yet to find peace with God and the rift amongst my relatives is still strong. Your prayers for salvation, healing and reconciliation would be really appreciated.

Alison is available to share more of her story at a more personal level, in the local church, ladies groups or at seminars. If you would like to do this or if you've simply been encouraged by her story, please feel free to contact her at; ali@alisonbuttenshaw.com

SALVATION PRAYER

If you have read this book but have not made the decision yet to become a Christian, it's as simple as praying the following prayer:

"Dear Lord, I admit that I am a sinner and have done many things that don't please you. I have lived my life for myself. I am sorry and I repent. I ask you to forgive me. I believe that you died on the cross for me to save me. You did what I could not do for myself. I come to you now and ask you to take control of my life. I give it all to you. Help me to live every day in a way that pleases you. In Jesus name, amen!"

What now?

Tell someone! You have made one of the most important decisions a person can ever make. It is worth celebrating!

Find a church. This is where you will be encouraged, inspired and motivated to be all that God wants you to be.

Buy a Bible and **read** it! It will give you hope when feeling hopeless, strength when feeling weak and courage when feeling afraid.

CHRISTIANS
AGAINST POVERTY

I'm passionate about loads of things in life – but if I could summarise it in one sentence, I'm passionate about seeing people set free. I want to see people healed from their past, hope restored for their future and the freedom to embrace **everything** that God has in store for them.

As mentioned earlier in my book, I now have the amazing privilege of working for Christians Against Poverty and have worked for them both in the UK and here in Australia.

Christians Against Poverty (CAP) is an international charity that is releasing people from debt and poverty through professional debt counselling, practical services and financial education.

CAP is an evangelical organisation that works in partnership with the local church. They are committed to helping anyone who is facing hardship as a result of financial difficulty and provide all of its services free of charge. With plans to have over 500 centres in the UK, 150 in Australia plus many more globally, this amazing charity is rapidly expanding and preparing to reach many more lives for Christ.

The three main reasons I personally love CAP are:-

1)   We are equipping the local church to meet the needs of its community. With over 11% of Australians living below the poverty line, CAP is empowering the church to effectively provide a solution.

2)   We are passionate about seeing families who are overwhelmed with financial difficulties offered hope and a sustainable solution.

3)   We are passionate about seeing clients freed from debt and free in Christ. Our motto is: "We are evangelists who do world-class debt counselling, not world-class debt counsellors who do evangelism."

Since opening the doors here in Australia, CAP in partnership with local churches has helped over 7,000 families! Over 800 clients have now accepted Christ and thousands of others are being helped though our debt prevention program, CAP Money.

Our vision is for every person in Australia, to have access to our life-transforming work by the year 2021! In order for this vision to become a reality we need approximately 150 full debt counselling centres and up to 1000 churches running the CAP Money course.

If you would like to find out more information about how you or your church can get involved, please contact our Partnership Department on (02) 4914 0597.

Christians Against Poverty (Australia) – www.capaust.org

Christians Against Poverty (UK) – www.capuk.org

Christians Against Poverty (New Zealand) – www.capnz.org